Bereavement Dreaming *and the* Individuating Soul

Bereavement Dreaming
and the Individuating Soul

GERI GRUBBS

NICOLAS-HAYS, INC.
Berwick, Maine

First published in 2004 by
Nicolas-Hays, Inc.
P. O. Box 1126
Berwick, ME 03901-1126
www.nicolashays.com
Distributed to the trade by
Red Wheel/Weiser, LLC
P. O. Box 612
York Beach, ME 03910-0612
www.redwheelweiser.com

Excerpt from "The Dead Woman" by Pablo Neruda on page 75 is from *The Captain's Verses*,
copyright © 1972 by Pablo Neruda and Donald D. Walsh. Reprinted by permission of
New Directions Publishing Corp.

LIBRARY OF CONGRESS CATALOGING-IN-PUBLICATION DATA
Grubbs, Geri A.
Bereavement dreaming and the individuating soul / Geri A. Grubbs.
p. cm.
ISBN 0-89254-079-6 (pbk. : alk. paper)
1. Death in dreams. 2. Grief. 3. Bereavement–Psychological aspects.
4. Individuation (Psychology) I. Title
BF1099.D4 G78 2004
155.9'37--dc22 2003025439
VG
Cover and text design by Kathryn Sky-Peck
Typeset in 11/14 Centaur
Printed in the United States of America
10 09 08 07 06 05 04
7 6 5 4 3 2 1

The paper used in this publication meets the minimum requirements of the
American National Standard for Information Sciences—
Permanence of Paper for Printed Library Materials Z39.48–1992 (R1997).

To my dear son, Michael,
who engaged with me in the meeting place between life and death.

CONTENTS

ACKNOWLEDGMENTS

M y first acknowledgment is to the universal soul that drove me at a crucial time in my life to analyze the bereavement dreams I had long forgotten, written in the pages of my journal. Words, "the fate of Gilgamesh," rang in my mind upon awakening the morning after I intuitively knew I had to analyze those dreams. I had no idea what or who Gilgamesh was. Then, synchronistically, I found myself reading through the pages of the ancient Babylonian epic of Gilgamesh that detailed the hero's courageous descent into the underworld and his search for immortality following the tragic death of his dear friend. These words, "the fate of Gilgamesh," guided me to also journey into the underworld—not in search of immortality, but for the herb of renewed life.

Many noble people responded to my advertised request for the sharing of their dreams following a tragic death of an intimate loved one. I am immensely grateful for their open-heartedness in sending me these very personal dreams. Three of them, Sarah, Joan, and Susan, worked closely with me in the processing of their dreams. Their stories are contained within my diploma thesis at the C. G. Jung Institute in Zurich. Sarah continued to work with me in the present book, along with Peter and Kathleen. Words cannot express the gratitude I feel for these five generous souls who shared their most profound moments of grief and inner wisdom with me. Without them, this book would never have been written.

I am also immensely thankful for the support and feedback of my thesis committee at the Jung Institute in Zurich: Andreas Schweizer, Art Funkhouser, and Francoise O'Kane. They were a strong presence many years ago when my work on bereavement had just begun. Many thanks to my colleague, Terrill Gibson, who took the time to read my manuscript and pass on his expertise. Finally, I send my love and appreciation to my husband, Ed, for his unremitting devotion, and to my dear daughter, Cora, for being the strong presence that she is in my life and for sharing with me her journey as an author and mother.

Of him I love day and night I dream'd I heard he was dead,
And I dream'd I went where they had buried him I love, but he was not
  in that place,
And I dream'd I wandr'd searching among buried-places to find him,
And I found that every place was a buried-place;
The houses full of life were equally full of death, (this house is now,)
The streets, the shipping, the places of amusement . . . were as full of the dead
  as the living,
And fuller, O vastly fuller of the dead than of the living;
And what I dream'd I will henceforth tell to every person and age,
And I stand henceforth bound to what I dream'd,
And now I am willingly to disregard burial places and desperse with them,
And if the memorials of the dead were put up indifferently everywhere, even in
  the room where I eat or sleep, I should be satisfied,
And if the corpse of any one I love, or if my own corpse, be duly render'd to
  powder and pour'd in the sea, I shall be satisfied,
Or if it be distributed to the winds I shall be satisfied.

—WALT WHITMAN, *Leaves of Grass*

INTRODUCTION

Millions of Americans today have such a deep need to contact their deceased loved ones that the business of mediumship has taken hold as never before. Famous mediums like James Van Praagh and Sylvia Browne have had books on the *New York Times* bestseller list for years and often use their psychic abilities with large audiences of hopefuls waiting to hear from their deceased loved ones. According to a 1994 *USA Today*-CNN-Gallup poll, almost seventy million of us believe it is possible to communicate with the dead. The afterlife business is, therefore, booming, with sales of books, tapes, movies, and TV programs skyrocketing.[1]

This need to connect with the dead, especially following the loss of a loved one, is innate. It has been with us since time immemorial, despite modern attempts to suppress it. What people instinctively sense about the dead transcends anything doubting skeptics or logically-minded thinkers may assert. Twenty-five years ago, when interest in the paranormal and life after death was at a low point, Jungian analyst Aniela Jaffé investigated the results of a question presented by the editor of a Swiss newspaper. In response to a series of articles on prophetic dreams, coincidences, premonitions, and apparitions, the editor inquired if readers had had similar experiences. He received 1,200 letters containing 1,500 accounts of personally-experienced parapsychological phenomena.[2]

A 1990 study on what constitutes normal bereavement following the loss of a spouse found that up to 42 percent encountered loved ones in dreams, while 71 percent felt their presence. Those studied often heard or saw the dead, or experienced *haptic* (touching) sensations. Sometimes, they felt their loved ones hovering over them in a watchful way. Close to 35 percent frequently communicated with the deceased, even as long as thirteen months following death.[3] Bereavement counselors consider all of these experiences in the context of normal reality testing and a healthy adaptation to a loss by death.

People want and need to bring closure to their relationships with deceased loved ones, especially when a sudden tragedy takes them away in an instant. They long to know how they are and if their souls are, indeed, in another realm of existence, as so many religions teach and paranormal phenomena indicate. Today, however, this desire has become especially strong? Why? Is it because our Western way of thinking has consigned us to such spiritual emptiness that we must search for completion wherever we can find it? Or is it that we instinctively long to have a relationship with the divine and sense that, with the passing of loved ones, we can enter this realm? Are we looking for our departed to confirm our belief in other dimensions of existence? Or do we have unfinished business to resolve and yearn to be with our loved ones to redress relationships at which we failed when they were alive?

Contracting with a medium to contact a departed loved one is tricky business. You must put your faith in the hands of another, rather than have direct contact yourself. There is also doubt about the credibility and reputation of mediums who do what are called "cold readings," generalized statements that apply to everyone who grieves. Yet, you are comforted when hearing from your departed loved one, even when it is through another. It is the only way that we, as Westerners, know.

In this book, I will show you another, more personal, way of hearing from and communing with your loved ones after death—through your nightly dreams. The power of dreams has been acknowledged and documented—even through writings etched on stone tablets—for thousands of years. Religious leaders and prophets, great leaders of ancient cultures, and indigenous peoples of the Earth have all used this inner dimension to answer personal and universal problems, share transcendent experiences, and connect with generations past.

My first personal experience with death and the beyond occurred twenty years ago, when my son Michael died in a tragic and uncanny encounter with another boy his age. Struck from behind, he fell, face forward, onto a concrete walk. My outer life returned to "normal" after his funeral, but my internal world remained disconnected for months afterward. I had been recording my dreams for years before Michael's death, so I was well aware that they had become profoundly different during the months following his death. Not only did they express my pain, they also showed me a new dimension of reality— that "other" place in which my son now existed. It was that world that communicated the true reality of my state of being at the time: visions of Michael living in another place and time, grossly vivid aspects of the death and transformation of matter, and illuminations that could be called "transcendent." Since I had no training or experience in working with dreams at that time, I could only record them and allow myself to experience the emotional impact they had on my internal world and everyday life. At times, these strange dreams took me to a spaceless-timeless dimension that I had not known before. At other times, I felt the strong impact of death more than ever.

Ten years later, as a candidate at the C. G. Jung Institute in Zurich, I analyzed the dreams that, in many ways, helped me survive those years of painful bereavement. In my analysis, I found that the dreams contained many images of death rituals from ancient religious traditions, continuous searching for a son who was (and then was not) dead, out-of-body experiences, and personal grief issues I needed to face. During the first two months, the dreams were specifically transcendental. Then they gradually became more personal and outer-life oriented. For a good two years, I dreamed heavily of my son at various ages. Thirteen years following his death, I finally resolved the intense conflict we were in at the time he died. Michael then became an image of guidance for me, appearing in my dreams when I was again faced with loss in my life through the death of my mother. It was obvious to me that our relationship continued beyond the grave, through good times and bad, as it would have had he lived. In my dreams, however, Michael became co-mingled with the powers that were beyond my everyday, earthly existence. He became a clear image of my soul's longing for that other dimension that we call transcendent.

Ancient civilizations appreciated the wisdom of dreams and used them often for guidance and emotional, physical, and spiritual healing. Written accounts of dreams and the gifts they bring from the spirit world are abundant in the Old Testament. Jacob's dream is a prominent example. While in deep sleep, Jacob saw a vision of a ladder that connected his sleeping body to the heavens above. Upon this ladder, he saw a procession of angels ascending and descending. Such an image suggests the profound nature of the dream process and how it connects us to universal or heavenly realms of consciousness.

The practice of incubation, or dream seeking, for the purpose of healing and communion with the deceased was actively cultivated in ancient Mesopotamia, Greece, Rome, Egypt, and China. Clay tablets and papyri from those times contain dream-work techniques, symbol dictionaries, and descriptions of personal dreams that produced the healing desired. In Greece, dream incubation that involved elaborate preparatory procedures and prayers to dream deities was a prominent and successful form of physical and emotional treatment. In the second century B.C., there were over 300 active temples in Greece and the Roman Empire dedicated specifically to Aesculapius, the well-known god of healing. Often, he appeared in dreams that were incubated to reveal what healing method and medicine were required for the suffering soul. Hippocrates, the father of present-day medicine, emphasized the importance of dreams to healing. He taught that dreams could diagnose illnesses, provide psychological help, and give soul support for past and future events not yet known by the dreamer. In Egypt, professional dream interpreters called oracles, "the learned men of the magic library," lived and worked in dream temples, just as contemporary doctors work in hospitals.

Many cultures, including the Egyptian, Hebrew, Chinese, and Tibetan, believe that the soul travels out of the body during sleep and interacts with other realms of consciousness. The Egyptian soul, referred to as *Ba*, is depicted in paintings as a human-headed bird that is said to remain conscious and active in the afterlife. The Chinese soul, *hun*, is considered closely connected with the dream process, travels out-of-body during sleep, and communes with the souls of the dead. It was not unusual for the Chinese to sleep on gravesites to incubate a dream of the deceased.

The place of dreams, then, is the meeting place between life and death. Dreams cross the realm of sleep for the living and the place of death for the deceased. Encounters with deceased spirits in dreams are not uncommon, even in Western society. Such encounters, sometimes called visitations, occur for several months or even years following a loss by death. Even during the day, thoughts from a deceased loved one may suddenly come upon you, as if from another place. It is only in your dreams, however, that you have emotional and apparent physical contact with them. Mental health and bereavement counselors affirm that after-death interactions such as these are a valid means of working through grief. Only in dreams can meetings with the dead be so vividly real and give a deep sense of peace and comfort to those who grieve.

In the following chapters, you will meet and journey with Gilgamesh, the mythical hero who, through the death of his intimate friend, went in search of immortality and returned as a transformed hero king. You will explore funerary rites in indigenous cultures and hear about past research into transcendent states of consciousness, referred to by the Tibetans as "the meeting place between life and death." You will learn about the many stages of bereavement dreaming, and especially dreams referred to as "translimi-nal," in which the souls of the dead and the living meet. You will share four dream journeys of the bereaved, from the closest and most intimate family tie between mothers and their deceased children, to a less intimate, but significantly meaningful, kinship between two brothers, one who died to leave a fateful calling within the dreams of the other. You will see how wives and husbands, mothers and children interact in the dream world when one has died suddenly, and how they bring closure and then transformation to a relationship tragically severed in physical life. Included in these dream stories is my personal journey, which commenced with a prophetic dream eighteen months before my son's death. The dreams that I had following his death cover a period of fourteen years and reveal the many stages of our relationship—from his objective presence as a spirit soul to an internalization of his reality within my psychic being.

Finally, you will journey to the Mexican South where death transcends boundaries and expands upon and becomes intermingled with life on Earth in an annual celebration called *el Dia de los Muertos* (Day of the Dead). You will experience the lights and aura of the dead as you observe families communing in celebration with their departed loved ones. To them, it is natural to commune with their dead through ritual and celebration. I hope that, from them and the stories that you read, you too will learn to be more comfortable with, and related to, your departed loved ones.

Part One

UNDERSTANDING DEATH

chapter one

BY WAY OF GILGAMESH

Your pain is the breaking of the shell that encloses your understanding.
Even as the stone of the fruit must break, that its heart may stand in the sun,
so must you know pain.

—KAHLIL GIBRAN, *The Prophet*

One of the first dreams ever recorded was painstakingly etched on clay tablets over 4,000 years ago in ancient Babylonia. The dream was a death prophecy in what is now referred to as *The Gilgamesh Epic*. *The Gilgamesh Epic* is a significant myth because it portrays a process that many who grieve undertake, the universally experienced search for immortality and the purpose of existence.

As with most myths, the significance of *The Gilgamesh Epic* is based in the culture that produced it. The ancient Babylonians believed that death was an end to human existence, but Gilgamesh, in shock over the sudden death of his soul mate, Enkidu, was driven to prove otherwise by journeying into the depths of the underworld. On this legendary journey, he courageously overcomes the tremendous obstacles set before him by the gods and faces death many times over. His quest is to find the one human ordained immortal by the gods—Utnapishtim, the only human who had survived the ultimate fate of death and could thus tell him its secret. At the end of this courageous journey, Gilgamesh returns to his kingdom transformed. Armed with his newfound acceptance of death, he becomes a wiser and more compassionate ruler who knows the mystery of life in that other world.

In the first part of *The Gilgamesh Epic*, generally associated with the first part of life, the hero-god of the Sumerian people of Babylonia accomplishes many things as King, but his rule is harsh and overbearing. Out of great anguish, the people petition the gods for help. In response, they are given Enkidu, an uncivilized wild man with potentially divine qualities. Attracted by Enkidu, Gilgamesh seduces him in the darkness of the forest and soon they become inseparable friends. Enkidu is Gilgamesh's animal soul, that which must be assimilated in order for Gilgamesh, as ruler, to become whole.

The first part of this grand epic involves a good deal of detail about Gilgamesh's taming and education of Enkidu, followed by their daring quest to overcome Ishtar, the Great Mother. Metaphorically, this is what we all must do during the first half of our lives—accept the challenge of being human without identifying with what we see as the grandness of our egos. Having encountered this, Gilgamesh is confronted with a tragedy that is more horrible to bear than any he has faced thus far—the sudden death of his soul mate, Enkidu, the one who made him whole. Through an act ordained by the gods, he must now come to terms with the impact of the ultimate reality of death on his very human existence. This fateful death is shown to Enkidu in a dream, in which he hears the gods in council discussing what will take place: ". . . Enlil said: 'Enkidu shall die; Gilgamesh shall not die!'"[1]

As ordained by the gods, Gilgamesh faces the harsh reality of a tragic loss by death. In anguish, he pleads for things to be different.

> My brother, my dear brother, why do they acquit me instead
> of thee?
> . . . Shall I sit down by the spirit of the dead,
> At the door of the spirit of the dead?
> And shall I never again see my dear brother with mine eyes?[2]

Like the mythical Gilgamesh, you also react to the loss of what helped you feel whole—a child, spouse, intimate friend, lover. You sense that life has dealt you a horrible blow, especially with the loss of a child. You see your expected destiny reversed, as if the child were capriciously taken from you by the hand of God. It goes against the established order when a parent buries a child. As the one who remains, you agonize over why your dearest and most precious had to die, wondering if there is any reason to go on in the face of such a fate.

A new summons enters Gilgamesh's life after he bravely undertakes the hero's journey with his animal soul, Enkidu. By joining with Enkidu and then losing him, Gilgamesh confronts the painful reality of mortality and begins his journey in quest of possibile immortality and the meaning and purpose of existence.

> He touched his heart, but it did not beat.
> Then he veiled his friend like a bride . . .
> He lifted his voice like a lion,
> Like a lioness robbed of her whelps.
>
> . . . .
>
> I will clothe myself with the skin of a lion and
> will roam over the desert.[3]

Such a loss creates a turning point in your life, and there is no choice but to go through the agonizing experience that seems ordained by the gods. In this archetypal experience of death, you are plunged into such intense suffering and emotion that you may feel as if a large chunk of your heart has been violently wrenched from your chest, leaving a gaping hole that never stops hurting. Such pain cannot be communicated to others. You may bury it beneath layers of defenses in order to cope in your everyday world, but somehow, you manage to go on because, deep within your soul, you are supported by something greater than yourself. To be touched by tragic loss is to be touched by something greater, a divine source that comes from the collective soul of humanity.

This painful experience can leave you few choices. You are touched and, because of that, are forced either to journey inward and face an unknown battle, or die a psychological death in the outer world, which, time and again, returns to remind you that all is not well. As Jung said: "Accepting death is the condition for reaching new life. If one does not accept death, one gets [a psychological] death."[4]

In the myth of Gilgamesh, the chronicler tells us:

> Gilgamesh for Enkidu, his friend,
> Weeps bitterly and roams over the desert.
> "When I die, shall I not be like unto Enkidu?
> Sorrow has entered my heart.
> I am afraid of death and roam over the desert."[5]

The desert is synonymous with the underworld. Gilgamesh is afraid of death and roams, not by choice, but out of necessity, in the place of the dead. "Death is dwelling in my bedchamber," he mourns, "and wherever I set my feet there is death!"[6]

The stark reality of mortality strikes Gilgamesh to the core as he wanders through the desert plains, crying bitterly over the death of his dear friend. Out of profound anguish, he searches for Utnapishtim, the only human who can help him—one who has become eternal with the gods. While on his quest, he experiences the Night Sea Journey, which takes him into many strange, archaic lands and dangerous waters. He confronts death and rebirth again and again. Courageously, he finds the large lions, then comes upon the Scorpion People, guardians at the Gate of the Mountain. He tells them:

> Though it be in sorrow and pain,
> In cold and heat,
> In sighing and weeping, I will go!
> Open now the gate of the mountains.[7]

The Scorpion People, husband and wife, keep watch over the rising and setting of the sun. The scorpion is the astrological symbol of death and rebirth, and therefore personifies the main purpose of Gilgamesh's journey through the mountain to the other side,[8] something that no mortal has ever sought before. Yet the "Man-Scorpion" not only allows him to cross, he directs his way. The divine in you that leads you to follow the sun is like the two-thirds divine in Gilgamesh, which guides him and helps him overcome all obstacles. Mythological heroes are partly human and at least half divine, a representation of your divine nature.

Gilgamesh follows the sun's road to its rising and into the mountain's twelve leagues of darkness. As he encounters the twelve leagues, or the Dark Night of the Soul, they envelop him more and more completely until, by the ninth league, he cries out in deep agony. Finally, by the tenth league, he feels the north wind on his face and, in the eleventh, the light of dawn appears. At the twelfth, the sun streams out and he sees the garden of the gods, "where trees bear jewels as fruit, lapis lazuli and carnelian," all symbols of the Self.[9] With help from Siduri the Barmaid, who dwells by the edge of the sea, and Urshanabi, the boatman who guides him over the Waters of Death,

Gilgamesh finally meets Utnapishtim, the Old Wise Man who can help him find everlasting life. After much insistence by Gilgamesh, Utnapishtim finally gives him that which he seeks—the divine secret of the gods:

> Gilgamesh, thou hast come hither, thou hast become weary, thou
> hast exerted thyself,
> What shall I give thee wherewith thou mayest return to thy land?
> Gilgamesh, I will reveal unto thee a hidden thing,
> Namely, a secret of the gods will I tell thee:
> There is a plant like a thorn . . .
> Like a rose, its thorn will prick thy hand.
> If thy hands will obtain that plant, thou wilt find new life.[10]

Gilgamesh is told where to find, not immortality, but the plant for renewed life, a plant that can be harvested in the depths of the water. He goes to the water:

> He tied heavy stones to his feet;
> They pulled him down into the deep, and he saw the plant.
> He took the plant, though it pricked his hands.
> He cut the heavy stones from his feet,
> And the . . . [sic] threw him to its shore.
> Gilgamesh said to him, to Urshanabi, the boatman:
> "Urshanabi, this plant is a wondrous plant,
> Whereby a man may obtain his former strength."[11]

With his precious find, Gilgamesh eagerly journeys home. On his way, he stops to bathe in a pool of water, leaving the plant on the shore. Perceiving its fragrance, a serpent emerges from the water, snatches the plant of renewed life, and takes it down into the water's depths, shedding its skin as it returns to the bottom. Gilgamesh weeps with agony upon seeing the precious plant, for which he journeyed long and hard, disappear back into the depths of the water. Unbeknownst to him, however, a new and glorious event has occurred. The capacity of the snake, a representative of unconscious life, to shed its skin has created a change in the collective unconscious of humankind. The serpent sheds its skin as it takes the herb of renewal back into the depths. Such a process represents the regeneration of life itself and is a profound symbol of transformation and renewal.

Gilgamesh returns to Uruk with his friend, Urshanabi, a divine figure intimately related to death. He returns as a transformed man-king, one who has survived the Night Sea Journey and knows from experience the land of the dead and the secret behind the immortality of the gods. Gilgamesh no longer harbors the ego-pride of his previously driven nature, but is linked in a greater way to the divine within him. Through the experiences encountered on his journey of the Dark Night of the Soul, Gilgamesh has changed. As Kluger aptly states: ". . . he came to know the 'secrets of the gods,' . . . found the herb of life, . . . saw the light he longed to see, and felt the spirit he had missed."[12]

Gilgamesh is transformed as a result of Enkidu's life and death because he bravely encounters his own questions about death. He may fail in his attempt to gain immortality, but he does not fail to find new meaning for himself here on Earth. The lesson for us is that you must first accept death before you can live a fully meaningful life, just as you must learn to accept and internalize the death of your dear love before you can become a whole and caring being.

When death strikes so deeply and personally, it becomes what Jungians call "an archetypal experience." Such an experience "gets its full weight only when it meets in us the maturity to receive and to understand it."[13] What does this mean? An archetypal experience is one that is shared, in a spiritual sense, by all members of the human race. Archetypes are soul material, spiritual energy that arises from the depths of your being. They are, in many ways, connected to realms of existence that are not of this Earth. Thus, to experience the death of a loved one is to experience an archetype that challenges you to change and become a more complete human being. Such a change requires a conscious decision to experience emotional pain fully and question the images of death that come to you through your dreams and fantasies.

True, Gilgamesh did not find immortality or peace of mind, just as you cannot revive your dead love in a purely physical way. There is no immortality here on Earth. But there is peace and resolution in the hereafter. As a result of his journey into the hereafter, Gilgamesh's spirit changed. He returned to life on Earth with a newfound acceptance of death that made him a wiser and more compassionate ruler. When you face the death of a loved one rather than run away from it, you also experience the divine. Gilgamesh's journey is a mythical drama of the journey every person in bereavement must make. By facing your darkest traumas, you too are transformed.

Gilgamesh's journey is the bereaved's symbol of transformation from a tragic encounter with death. His odyssey represents what Jungians refer to as a process of individuation, one specifically brought on by a shattering event in the second part of life. Individuation is your journey toward wholeness, or the realization of your greater personality. It is the fulfillment of your true destiny or birthright. To become individuated is to realize your Self, or soul, and then to fully express it in the outer world in productive and fulfilling ways.

Jung identifies two main phases in the individuation process. In the first, you become conqueror of your domain. You develop an ego identity, find worthwhile relationships and professional ideals, and essentially make your life on Earth meaningful. In the second phase, or middle years of life, you confront a major task that challenges your divine nature. This task taxes your ego attachments by calling into doubt your many accomplishments, your material gratification, and the identity you have created. This phase is one often associated with the Dark Night of the Soul. Loss of a loved one is the ultimate of these tasks, one which, when confronted, leaves you forever changed. To become whole as an individual, especially when faced with the harsh reality of a loved one's death, you must come to terms with death. Life demands this of you.

chapter two

LIMINALITY
AND TRANSCENDENCE

This possible transcendence of space-time, for which it seems to me there is a good deal of evidence, is of such incalculable import that it should spur the spirit of research to the greatest effort . . . the psyche's attachment to the brain, i.e., its space-time limitation, is no longer as self evident and incontrovertible as we have hitherto been led to believe.

—C. G. JUNG, *Collected Works*, vol. 8, ¶813

In the tiny Greek village of Potamia, a child has died. Following the village's Christian Orthodox tradition, the child's body is buried in a wooden box and allowed to decompose naturally for five years. To benefit the needs of the soul in this five-year period of transition, the women of the family visit the grave daily and memorial services are performed on significant anniversary dates. The women occasionally talk about how the needs of the dead are communicated to them in their dreams. Lamps and candles are placed on the grave and lit as a prayer for salvation.

In an elaborate and final ritual on the fifth anniversary of the death, the body of the child is exhumed and placed in its final resting place in a shelter with the community's ancestral bones. This event marks the end of the liminal period of mourning, when both the remains of the deceased and those in mourning emerge from their darkness to enter a new state of being. The dead depart the blackness of the Earth; the living shed their black garments. Both are lightened by departing from the weight and pain of the liminal state of being.[1]

Although this may seem like a bizarre practice from a Western point of view, it is performed regularly in many cultures throughout the world, some in North and South America. This important rite of transition reminds the community that, as the body decomposes, the soul journeys to its final destination in the afterlife. It is believed that this takes from several months to many years, allowing for the souls of the deceased and the bereaved to have a smooth transition from one state of being to another. From a theoretical point of view, the purpose of such an extensive and elaborate rite of passage is threefold: it marks the separation of the soul from the body and the dead from the living, allows for a supportive transition of the soul into the realm of the dead, and provides for a gradual transition of the bereaved back into society.[2]

Cultural anthropologist Arnold van Gennep has observed that passages are not instantaneous events, but gradual processes of transition from one state of being to another that certainly require a time of adjustment. Primitive cultures allow for this through the celebration of initiation rites. Passages of life share a common structure:

- Separation, or removal from a previously occupied state;
- Transition, or the state of liminality, the period of being neither here nor there;
- Final integration of the soul or psyche into a new state of being.

Van Gennep's theory can be applied to many life passages, including birth, marriage, and death. On the subject of funerals, he states:

One expects rites of separation to be the most prominent component. A study of the data, however, reveals that the rites of separation are few in number and very simple, while the transition rites (from one state of being to another) have a duration and complexity sometimes so great that they must be granted a sort of autonomy.[3]

The bereaved enter a transitional, or liminal, period following a sudden separation by death, and the liminal period they experience is revealed in their dreams. In Eastern religions, it is believed that this liminal period coincides with the transitional period of the deceased, and that they both terminate when the deceased's spirit is incorporated into the world of the dead. How long this liminal period lasts depends, in large part, on the closeness of their relationship and its complexity at the time of the death.[4]

THE TRANSCENDENTAL REALM OF CONSCIOUSNESS

For more than thirty years, Stanislav Grof researched supra-ordinary states of consciousness induced by psychedelic drugs and nonpharmacological methods, most notably, holotropic breath work.[5] Based upon his research, Grof defined what he saw as four dimensions of the human psyche:

- The physically oriented sensory barrier;
- The individual unconscious with its life experiences, traumatic memories, and unresolved conflicts;
- The parenatal and spiritual realm;
- The transpersonal realm that transcends the limitations of time and space.

In this last dimension, the extension of consciousness appears to go beyond earthly existence in space and time and contain images of deceased spirits, archetypes, religious entities, demons, and mythological forms. Grof claims it is critically important to take this realm into consideration when seriously exploring experiences of psychedelic states, shamanism, religion, mysticism, rites of passage (liminality), mythology, parapsychology, and schizophrenia.[6] I would add to this list the dream state following a loss by death, because that state, too, becomes a spaceless and timeless dimension, as we shall see later in the dream stories of the bereaved.

When you are in a transpersonal dimension of the psyche, you transcend the usual limitations of consciousness, go beyond linear time or ordinary spatial boundaries, and experience domains that are not considered part of your everyday reality. In this state, you encounter an otherworldly consciousness[7] that becomes a condition of the liminal state of grief. Jung speaks of this when he says:

> Naturally we can form no conception of a relatively timeless and spaceless existence, but, psychologically, and empirically, it results in manifestations of the continual presence of the dead and their influence on our dream life. I therefore follow up such experiences with

the greatest attention, because they show many things we dream about in a very peculiar light, where "psychological" structures appear as existential conditions.[8]

It is not unusual for the spirit of the deceased to return in a dream to a dear one with the apparent purpose of describing what it is like for him or her in this transcendent place. A man who lost his brother quite suddenly had a vivid dream of a visit with him several months after his death. The dream is significant in that it appears to address the alchemy of the soul's crossing to another dimension of reality.

I had been hanging out with Andrew in some way, but now it was time for him to go. I joined him as he headed up to the third floor where he would "pass over." It occurred to me "Why should I say goodbye here?" I asked him if I could walk with him and he said "No problem." I didn't intend to watch him pass over; I was just seeing him to the "door." He had a sextant-like tool he looked through to align things. It was metal, coated in black. I saw two glasses of liquid, which he told me were needed to make the process work. I think one was distilled water and the other was like a chemical from a photographer's darkroom. I let him know how unsettled I was that this process was so tenuous. What if he ran out of these liquids? "Oh well . . . that'd be it," seemed his response. I asked what I could do. He said "Get more of those liquids and tell Mom that she was right about that music, that this one particular CD was as close as earthly music could come to mimic. At that moment, he "left" in the iridescent mist. I averted my eyes to give him privacy, not curious at all.

Is Andrew trying to show his brother the indescribably blissful quality of that "other" dimension? He says that the music we have on Earth only mimics what he experiences in the hereafter. Through his use of the sextant-like tool and two liquids, Andrew demonstrates the precise and tenuous nature of crossing from what appears to be the third to the fourth dimension. Certainly, this passing is a mystery. What Andrew demonstrates is complicated and can provide only a photographic view of life after death.

Edward Edinger claims that "dreams do reveal, to some extent, the 'mystery of being.' . . . [and] can properly be called metaphysical, i.e., beyond the physical or ordinary conceptions of life."[9] These dreams are different from ordinary dreams and cannot be interpreted subjectively. A man with whom Edinger worked was unique in that he had attempted suicide just prior to seeing Edinger for treatment, and died of natural causes shortly after terminating treatment. About one-third of his dreams "had definite metaphysical or transcendental allusion," Edinger states. "Repeatedly I had the impression that the unconscious was trying to give the patient lessons in metaphysics— either to help him assimilate the meaning of his very close brush with death or to prepare him to meet death in the near future."[10]

Jung, Grof, von Franz, and Edinger are only a few of the many who have addressed this issue. The loss of a loved one, and especially that of a child, is a circumstance that surely thrusts you into the transcendent dimension of consciousness. Not only do you continue to feel and sense the image of your love who has crossed over, but you experience a state of liminality as well, a state that is spaceless and timeless, and open to the spiritual, archetypal, and collective realm of the depths of the unconscious.

A MEETING PLACE BETWEEN LIFE AND DEATH

When you experience a tragic loss by death, you enter a state of conscious-ness that can best be described as a "gap between two realities." You, along with the one you've lost, go through a kind of death. All of your feelings come to the surface, causing extreme anguish and even panic at times. In an especially tragic loss, these feelings are magnified and intensified. Tibetan Buddhists refer to this gap between two realities as a *bardo*, the counterpart of the state of liminality. Bardos are junctures in which dramatic change can happen, a place where the spirit can unite with something other than the physical world. Sogyal Rinpoche describes it as "a moment when you step toward the edge of a precipice."[11]

Tibetans believe that, when you are in the bardo state of deep sleep, your spirit or "subtle body" is free to wander in the place of the dead. They believe that you are actually in the condition of life after death while sleep-ing. Such a belief in the existence of the subtle body is an aspect of many cultures, particularly Buddhism, Hinduism, primitive societies, and Western spiritualism. The subtle body is the soul spirit that resides between mind and body, the spirit that wanders in the spaceless and timeless dimension of the psyche and the body of the soul after death. There is no evidence of the exis-tence of the subtle body from a Western point of view, except through para-psychological reports, but it has been talked about since early times. In the second century C.E., the great philosopher Plutarch described the souls of the dead as "surrounded by a flamelike bubble or covering; some are of the purest moonlight, sending out a soft, continuous color."[12]

According to the Tibetans, at the moment of death, the soul enters the bardo of death, a continuation of the soul's journey, or, as Jungians would say, the individuation process. The bardo period lasts forty-nine days, after which the soul enters another form of existence. During the first twenty-one of the forty-nine days, the soul of the deceased remains closely connected with the life just lived; during the last twenty-eight days, it is focused on the life to come. Immediately following death, the dead remain linked to their previous earthly existence, making communication easier between the deceased and those left behind. After that, contact becomes more difficult, but can still take place.

While in the bardo of death, the consciousness of the deceased is highly clairvoyant; they are able to see and hear the thoughts of their earthly counterparts. If the strife, anguish, and suffering of those left behind is strong, the deceased will naturally be affected by it. They too may plunge into deep grief. When a sudden death occurs, the deceased may not even realize that they are dead, and so may attempt to communicate with their loved ones.

There are definite characteristics to a dream visitation. In *Love Beyond Life*, Martin and Romanowski claim to have heard hundreds of these experiences, all of which have common hallmarks:

- The encounter is very meaningful to the dreamer, may answer an appeal for help and emotional support, and is remembered afterward in great detail.

- The deceased appear as they did in life, but tend to be much healthier physically and emotionally, and often appear younger than when they died.

- The dreams seem less disorganized and disjointed than dreams tend to be, are more vivid, persistent, and real, and are truly experienced as real visits.

- The message conveyed in the dream is simple and to the point, and the meaning of the dream appears obvious to the dreamer, in spite of what symbols may be present. For the dreamer, the visitation serves a specific purpose. The deceased may communicate something of importance about their condition after death, unfinished business with those they left behind, and may attempt to reestablish the bond that was broken so suddenly. In many cultures and religious traditions, it is believed that the dead bear messages meant to help the bereaved.

- The form of communication seems to be telepathic. Words are often minimal or nonexistent, yet the dreamer knows what was communicated, sensing that he or she was told very important information that cannot be recalled upon awakening.

- Information provided by the deceased is often verifiable. Details are described that the dreamer could not have known otherwise, such as future events, the whereabouts of lost items, or encounters with relatives not known personally.

- Dream visitations usually leave the dreamer with a strong feeling of peace and well-being.[13]

Following the death of his wife, Emma, Jung had a dream "that was like a vision."

> She stood at some distance from me, looking at me squarely. She was in her prime, perhaps about thirty, and wearing the dress which had been made for her many years before by my cousin the medium. It was perhaps the most beautiful thing she had ever worn. Her expression was neither joyful nor sad, but, rather, objectively wise and understanding, without the slightest emotional reaction, as though she were beyond the mist of affects. I knew that it was not she, but a portrait she had commissioned for me. It contained the beginning of our relationship, the events of fifty-three years of marriage, and the end of her life also. Face to face with such wholeness one remains speechless, for it can scarcely be comprehended.[14]

This is a classic dream visitation, whose purpose, I suspect, was to relieve Jung, albeit for a brief time, of his painful grief.

A deceased loved one continues to relate to you in your dreams and waking life as if they were still with you. It takes time for both you and the deceased to get used to the separation that so suddenly and drastically occurs in an unexpected death. Yet the relationship remains the same. If mother and child, or husband and wife, are in severe discordance or conflict prior to parting, the conflict between them continues in the dream state of the mother or spouse; if the relationship is dependent, it remains so after death. Conflicts left unresolved before death take on a similar form in the dreams of those left behind. Relationships very definitely continue beyond the grave, portraying in the dream state the love and communication between parties, the condition of the bereaved and the deceased, and unfinished business that remains to be completed.

chapter three

BEREAVEMENT DREAMING

The dead person is gone, and yet not gone. The intensity of this existential paradox creates an opening to the sacred: it is through our living emotional connection to the dead person that we are able to glimpse something of powers and realities that lie beyond our ordinary profane world. In these strangely vivid dreams, the dead person serves as a spiritual guide, leading the dreamer into realms that both frighten and fascinate the living. Who could be a better, more trustworthy guide into those mysterious realms than a person to whom we were close in life and who has just become a member of those realms?

—KELLY BULKELEY, *Spiritual Dreaming*

When you hear of the unexpected death of a loved one, you feel as though you are frozen in time. You disbelieve what is happening and everything around you seems unreal, as if you were living an endless nightmare. The physical world recedes into the background; you exist in a void or state of limbo, sensing that your life has become almost as dead as the one whom you've lost. These feelings begin the moment you hear of the death and remain for a week or two, sometimes months. As you tend to the final rites of the one so dear to you, close friends and relatives surround you with love and compassion, briefly lifting you from pain and anguish. Even if you used to dream frequently at night, you now seldom do. In fact, you are barely able to sleep, let alone dream.

Finally, the funeral and parting good-byes are over. Your family and friends leave to continue their lives as before, while you must face the dreadful emptiness of loss. Its reality hits you most deeply now, striking with a vengeance in the most profound pain you have ever experienced. You feel unbearably alone, trying as best you can to go on with life as it was before, as crazy as that may seem. Western society allows for little time to recover from such a loss.

If you have been aware of dreams before, you may find that they suddenly become intense and strangely different from other dreams you've had. Images of death and the one you've lost pervade your nighttime images, as if you have been drawn into the afterlife with him or her. You may have intimate encounters with your loved one, interacting together as you did before, as if nothing has changed. You may see spirits from the underworld, or be surrounded by death images from ancient cultures and religions. These dreams may confuse you, especially when you find yourself in a very real communion with your departed loved one. You may wonder how this can be, when that person is "dead and gone." If the dream visits continue, however, you may begin to look forward to them, because they provide you with the greatest possible respite from the throes of grief.

You may experience only one or two of these dreams, or you may have a series of them that continues, perhaps for a month or two during the first year following your loss. Many of these dreams take place during the phase of liminality and are highly transcendent. I refer to them as transliminal dreams, and to a continuous series of them as the transliminal dream state. Transliminal dreaming may provide you with soul support, or it may force you to face what you absolutely cannot otherwise face—the stark reality of what you have lost. It appears that the greater the isolation from others or the closer the relationship that was lost, the more intense the transliminal dream state. Compensation is also a factor in its intensity or length. If the outer world provides the spiritual support you need and you are facing all that you can face, you may not experience a transliminal dream state immediately after the death, nor will you have one if the death is not a severely tragic one. You may have one or two dreams that could be called transliminal, and these may be visitations from the deceased. Some of these dreams may come months, or even years, after the death.

CHARACTERISTICS OF TRANSLIMINAL DREAMS

The transliminal dream state has four major characteristics. First, symbols, archetypes, and the spirit of the deceased are more objective than subjective in nature in these dreams. Generally, dreams tend to be more subjective than objective, meaning that images and symbols within them are features of the dreamer's internal psychological situation. Jung describes subjective dreams as "a theater in which the dreamer is himself the scene, the player, the prompter, the producer, the author, the public, and the critic."[1] Everything in the dream—spouse, friend, or even physical items—is viewed as a partial self-object or aspect of the dreamer.

At times, however, dreams are more objective, meaning that the images in them come from your outer life situation, or from collective and universal situations. These dreams may address a relationship with a spouse, child, friend, or even a profession, giving you clues about a condition, problem, or relationship in the outer world. During times of transition, this objective orientation often addresses a collective or universal reality. Such dreams have a distinctly sacred quality to them, as if the dreamer were in communion with something profoundly greater than the mundane world of everyday life. Especially during times of crisis, loss, or dramatic life-changing events, dreams address basic existential questions concerning death, suffering, loss, and transformation. Often referred to as "big" dreams, these leave the dreamer with a sense of wonder and awe over their magnitude and are usually never forgotten.

The objective psyche is purely independent of personal reality. It is the realm that transcends the limitations of time and space, where the extension of consciousness goes beyond earthly existence. The objective realm contains images of deceased spirits, archetypes, religious entities, mythological figures, and even demons. Dreams that are objective or collective express a problem or issue that is universal rather than personal, a condition that all of humankind must, at some time, face. When in a state of bereavement— a universal condition—it presents death and dying and the relationship with the deceased spirit.

Shortly before making the final decision to study at the Jung Institute in Zurich, my inner Self was challenging me to make changes. I knew that my life had become stagnant and that I was being called to do something more with it. During that chaotic time, I had the following dream:

I talk my husband into going to therapy and go to meet him at a large building that appears to me to be the Jung Institute. It's an old building with many levels to it. I enter a large room and see various couples meeting in the open with their analysts. I am late and feeling frantic that I can't find my husband and our analyst. As I search for them, I find myself being drawn into a kind of sanctuary with a central, spiral staircase leading downward. I take the stairs and, as I walk down, I see an orange-and-gold-ringed mandala on the floor below me. It shines with a radiant light. In its center is a wrapped mummy lying on a bier. The bier and coffin seem to be coming up out of the circular rings. I'm mesmerized by what I see and can't take my eyes off of it

My dream is a good example of how you can move from a subjective to an objective reality within the same dream. In my analysis, or individuation process, I long to connect with my masculine essence, but I can't find it on the earthly level, nor in analysis. Instead, I am pulled to the sanctuary, or spiritual center of my being. As I walk down into the depths toward the collective unconscious, the dream takes on an objective reality. It turns profoundly mysterious and archetypal. I have definitely entered a sacred place where the archetypal world of the dead rises up to meet me. As transcendent dreams often do, this particular one has a distinctly prophetic quality to it. It was while studying at the Jung Institute one year later that I realized I was being called to explore, in depth, the dreams I had following the death of my son. It became a first step in an important life work that was to come.

The second characteristic of transliminal dreaming is that the dreamer feels truly in the presence of the deceased, and that, moreover, there is a purpose to their meeting. Suddenly they are together and may be in conversation about their parting. The setting may be familiar to them, or it may be in a spaceless-timeless place. If they are lovers, they may be embracing and loving each other as they had previously. Nothing seems different, although they may know that this meeting will not last. Emotions are intense and the dreamer may awaken with a wonderful sense of peace and comfort from having been with their deceased love; or the dreamer may feel troubled because the meeting did not last and only made the reality of death even more apparent.

One month following her husband's sudden death on a business trip, a woman had the following dream:

All of my senses were there on another plane with him that was just as real or more than this one. He had come back (from death?) but it was no big deal. Nobody mentioned it. We had a wonderfully fun quickie, a nooner. I could feel, taste, and smell him. Waking up was not a downer or depressing. I was floating on air for several days. It was as if I were just traveling back and forth between time-dimensional or different planes of existence. A Valentine's gift to show me he's still in my life?

Close to one month following the death of her 12-year-old son in a dirt-bike accident, Donna, a young mother dreamed:

I look outside the window to see a slender boy about 19 years old with sandy-colored hair coming out of a dark car with my son. They walk to the back of the house "to see the horses" someone says. Then I open the door and my son, Rory, walks into the house. I ask him who the other boy is and he says "Oh that's Tim Ruff" (couldn't hear that well—could have been Russ, Rush, or Rust). Rory hugs me tightly around the waist. It's electric feeling. I can smell him, feel him, see him—it's so very real.

After the dream, Donna was curious about "Tim Ruff," her son's escort, and immediately tried to identify him, to no avail. A week later, a strange feeling came over her when she was reading a book about bereaved parents and saw the name, "Tim Wresh." Donna knew that she had to investigate this name, which ultimately led her to the boy's parents. She found that Tim had died several years earlier of a heart defect and that his photo was similar to the boy in Donna's dream. Through Tim's parents, Donna was able to find comfort and support in a bereavement group. To this day, she believes that Rory brought Tim to her in her dream because of his concern over her grief.[2]

As evident in this profound situation, it is not unusual for the deceased to act as a spirit guide to the bereaved's recovery from grief and in their individuation process. They may communicate that emotions are too intense or that their loved one is not adequately facing the sudden loss. They may also warn about life-threatening issues or lead them, through dreams, into another existence of which the deceased is now a part. Such a situation occurred in the dream of a mother who lost her adult son in a death that was believed to have been a suicide:

My son is present in voice only. He tells me that the place between when I decide to go to sleep and when I actually fall asleep is the place where the dead are. It is my understanding that this is also the place of the "natural mind." He also presents an image of me in the driver's seat of his car and he is with me in the rider's seat like a cloud of vapor. He tells me that he will always be with me like this.

In transliminal dreaming, archetypes and symbols represented can easily be associated with funerary rites, and ancient religious and spiritual traditions. The tunnel of death often encountered in near-death experiences, the bridal or death chamber of Greek and Egyptian cultures, weddings of the deceased and the bereaved, dogs, cats, snakes, animals associated with the underworld, the recycling nature of plants, and the rebirthing process are only a few of the many images and themes dreamed by the bereaved. When encouraged to associate with these images, they usually are unable to do so because they appear as foreign to them as if they were from another world. Archetypes that emerge from the depths of the collective unconscious present a dimension of reality that is not an aspect of the dreamer; therefore, personal associations are difficult to make. The healing quality of these images do make an impression, however, which may be their intended purpose.

Deep in grief over the sudden death of her adult son, a mother dreams:

I am running with a group of people who are all wearing white. Suddenly, I stop because I see a coffin that I know I must prepare. The group is waiting for me to proceed with them, but I must prepare this coffin. It is wood in the shape of my son's coffin. There are sections inside of it, dividing it into quarters, the top being smaller, like a cross. I place a white flower at the four ends of the cross.

The coffin, quaternary, cross, and white flowers are significant in this dream because they are all representations of the process of death and transformation. The coffin and cross are replicas of the Tree of Life. In ancient Egypt, people were often buried in trees in memory of Osiris, the god of resurrection. The cross this mother tends by placing white flowers on it suggests redemption and victory through love and self-sacrifice. It appears that the mother's outwardly involved ego is drawn toward what death has brought into her life, a matter that requires her attention before she can go on with her spiritual activities in the outer world.

Two weeks following her fourteen-year-old daughter's sudden death in an auto accident, a mother dreams:

Michelle and I are walking along a dark alley when, suddenly, she falls down a rectangular hole. Feeling desperate to rescue her, I climb down the rocky face to get her. The climb into the hole is slow and scary, but I manage to do it. At the bottom, I find Michelle wearing her black model's dress. I'm surprised that it is not dark down here, but is instead filled with a deep, golden light. I think that we will both have to climb up the way I came down, but I see that, over to the right, there is a copper ladder fixed against the wall. We climb up—Michelle is behind me so I can't see her—and when we reach the top, two male helpers are there to help me out.

Susan, the mother, in desperate need to be with her daughter after her death, finds herself in a liminal place with her. She follows Michelle into a grave-like chamber, associated historically with the bridal chamber of death, and returns knowing that her daughter is nearby. This dream began a series of dreams for Susan that portrayed their involvement together in everyday life, as if Michelle were still alive.

Transliminal dreams also have a characteristic transcendent quality to them. There may be a numinous or spiritual aura to the images; the bereaved may have out-of-body experiences in the dream or intimate encounters with images of death.

Donna, the young mother who lost her 12-year-old son, Rory, dreams:

We're lying together on the floor on the front porch and Rory's face is in my lap. It's dark, but his face is very bright and shining. I'm thinking: "Look at the moonlight on his face," but there is no moonlight coming through the window.

A child of thirteen had the following dream shortly after her father's death from a heart attack:

I am in an enormous institutional restroom, looking for a place to hide. The room is brightly lit and has mostly white tile and porcelain fixtures. I am frantic for a place to hide; I feel pursued. Finally, I see a red satin curtain on one wall and I duck behind it. I find myself in a dark room. As I adjust to the darkness, I see that the room is full of open, empty coffins on biers. I hear someone in pursuit, so I jump into a coffin and close the lid. When it snaps shut, the bottom falls away and I drop down through the bier and the floor, and into a slide-like tunnel. I travel on my back at a great rate of speed, moving down, but also what feels like out and away from where I was. Eventually, my speed slows down and the end of the tunnel opens onto a river. I am in a coffin-shaped boat, sitting up and feeling uneasy, but enjoying the scenery. It is an overcast, warm, late-autumn day; the ground is covered with leaves. The river narrows, until eventually, it is scarcely wider than my boat. Ultimately, it narrows altogether and my boat bumps land. I get out on shore.

These two dreams reveal the transcendent quality of the spirit body of the deceased and how the bereaved can be engaged in intimate encounters with death. Such dreams are not only normal, they involve you in the process of healing and recovery from the pain of deep grief.

The transliminal state of dreaming, under normal circumstances, tends to be brief, averaging only one to two months. Transliminal dreaming is an intense state of psychic connection with the archetypal world of the dead brought on by a tragic loss. It appears to be meant as a time of support for the bereaved and for final good-byes which, when no longer needed, dissipates naturally and spontaneously. Indeed, if you remain in this transliminal state too long out of a preoccupation with the world of the dead, you risk an unresolved state of grief or, even worse, a loss of contact with reality. Jung speaks of this strongly when he advises an inquirer about contacting his dead brother in his dreams:

> . . . I would add that this [contact] is likely to be possible only as long as the feeling of the presence of the dead continues. But it should not be experimented with because of the danger of a disintegration of consciousness. To be on the safe side, one must be content with spontaneous experiences. Experimenting with this contact regularly leads either to the so-called communications becoming more and more stupid or to a dangerous dissociation of consciousness.[3]

Following is an example of a "warning" dream had by a woman who perhaps engaged herself too long with the spirits of the dead through her involvement in spirit groups:

I'm at my cousin's house and he is talking on the phone. When he hangs up, I ask him how his father is doing.

"Are you crazy—my father is dead!" he responds.

"That's fine—do you have a number I can call?"

"You are really out of your mind," he continues.

Suddenly, I'm driving up to a tollgate. It's gloomy and gray outside. Men are milling around and looking into the car—I'm feeling quite frightened. I see a large, old building—like a prison—in the distance. A male voice says that it's OK for me to go through. Next, I'm walking down the corridor of what seems to be an infirmary. A nurse is walking beside me. I ask to see my uncle and she leads me to the doorway. I see rows of beds and, way in the back, I see my uncle. I'm thrilled and wave hello to him.

"No, no," he says to me and waves me back.

I'm confused, but then find myself standing next to him, patting him on the back of his head, jumping up and down.

"Look, I'm here—can you see me, can you see me?" I say to him.

He smiles back.

It's quite clear that the dreamer in this situation can easily cross the barrier, or gateway, between the living and the dead, but is warned repeatedly that she should not do so. She walks down an infirmary, a place of illness, in which she can easily become imprisoned, since it also appears as a prison to her. Fear predominates in the dream, while the purpose of the visit remains unclear. It seems as though the dreamer plays with death rather than learns from it in any meaningful way. She enters a forbidden place to visit a relative out of fun, it seems, rather than through love and need. She is warned of such encounters by others in the dream, but does not heed the warnings. Two months later, she dreams:

I'm in a white space, a non-dimensional white room with no floor and no ceiling. Feeling anxious, I wonder where I am. I'm afraid that I'm going to see something frightening. Suddenly, a young man appears behind me out of nowhere. I'm startled and gasp as I turn to look at him. He smilingly says "hi" to me. Again I turn and see Mary, a deceased friend, zooming toward me with a bright smile on her face. Her face comes very close to mine and I wake up suddenly saying "Was that Mary, was that Mary?"

This woman plays with the dead, so the dead play with her for no apparent reason but to frighten her. The Tibetans believe that to be preoccupied with the dead or to hold on to a deceased loved one in a dependent relationship is unhealthy, not only for the living, but for the dead as well.[4] The continual presence of the dead in the dreams of the living is relative, since after several months, it naturally begins to taper off and eventually ends completely, although reappearances may occur during significant events or times of crisis for the living. When you maintain a preoccupation with the world of the dead or a dependent relationship with the deceased, a form of disconnectedness or dissociation results, as the previous dream reveals. There comes a point in the transliminal dream state when it is communicated by the spirit of the deceased, or in a symbolic way, that it is time to part. If you refuse to listen to the message and continue to hold on, severe emotional problems, or at least a serious state of unresolved grief, may occur.

Marie-Louise von Franz had what could be called a visitation dream three weeks after her father's death. In the dream, he arrived at her house, suitcase in hand. Much of her communication with him was telepathic, in that she and he both knew what was going to be said and what was going to happen as they thought it. After a brief "How are you?" and "What are you doing now?" conversation, the father said firmly and non-telepathically: "It is not good for either the dead or the living to be together too long. Leave me now. Good night."[5]

Often, the transliminal place itself contains barriers between the living and the dead. The departed may be separated from you by a glass, an invisible barrier, a river, or may tell you directly that they should not be touched. Jung claims that "the forms of existence inside and outside time are so sharply divided that crossing this boundary presents the greatest difficulties."[6]

In spite of this barrier, however, spirits of the departed and images of death come, in a very strong way, to those who have suffered a loss. Sometimes it cannot be avoided and at other times, it can easily be encouraged. Especially during the early phases of grief, praying and calling out to the departed love are often enough to precipitate a visit in a dream. It is important that you not become obsessed by this and that you accept whatever does or does not come. When your ego is overly involved in the realm of the dead, darkness, illness, and suffering can easily take hold. Prayer, love, and acceptance of what you are given or not given must be the overriding factor.[7]

PHASES OF THE BEREAVEMENT DREAM PROCESS

In their work with bereavement, therapists Lily Pincus and Beverley Raphael have observed a series of distinct phases that are a part of the bereavement process.[8] These phases include shock upon first hearing of the death, separation pain coupled with a period of searching and heightened emotions, and, finally, restitution and acceptance of the death. Verena Kast, in her book *A Time to Mourn*, adds a final phase that she defines as "a new relationship to oneself and the world."[9] In this phase, achieved primarily by those who work consciously toward individuation, the deceased becomes an internalized companion or a renewed soul quality of your being.

Through symbols and vivid imagery, dreams portray these emotional phases and usually provide compensation and respite. They also give you guidance as you complete unfinished business with your lost love, separating you from the life that you shared together and re-engaging in a life renewed. These phases usually take decades or even a lifetime to complete. Unless you are actively engaged in individuation through therapy, analysis, dream work, or spiritual practice, you may never bring them to a full resolution.

Shock and Disconnection

The state of dreaming tends to shut down on the days following a traumatic loss, similar to what has been observed on the emotional level. Disconnection is nature's way of protecting your psyche from a trauma that is too unbearable to experience emotionally. It is most pronounced when the death is sudden and unexpected and involves a very close love—a child, spouse, or intimate friend. Shock or disconnection under these conditions generally lasts a week or two, although they may continue for as long as a month in situations that are tremendously jarring to the psyche. Most likely, you will not dream while in this state, even if your dreams were abundant before the loss.

Family and close friends usually surround and support you at this time, which may distract you from the painful reality of what you are experiencing. You may feel as though you are living in a timeless dimension and that you have become a player in a nightmarish drama that will end when the funeral is over and everyone leaves. Instead, when they do leave, your nightmare continues and you most likely have to face it alone. It is at this moment that the stark reality of your loss becomes explicitly real—felt as an agonizing hole in the center of your heart that may easily cause you to panic at times. From this intense state, a dream may come to you suddenly in the middle of the night and in it you may find that, within your soul, you have become intimately engaged with the world of the dead.

Liminality

The transition from one state of being to another is a gradual process that begins with a sudden separation from a person or way of life and ends when you become integrated into a new way of being. Between these points of separation and renewal, you may drift in and out of a spaceless/timeless dimension of reality that is referred to by anthropologist Arnold van Gennep as a void or state of liminality,[10] or what the Tibetans call a *bardo*. Generally, when you are in this state, your ego is easily distracted from earthly matters and everyday life and is drawn to an other-world reality. You could say that a heightened state of awareness of this other world dominates your psyche, especially during dream and fantasy states. The psychic separation between the physical and transpersonal dimensions of reality is thin for the recently bereaved, allowing them to interact more easily than usual with spirit bodies, religious figures, and archetypal entities. It is not unusual to talk to loved ones telepathically, visit with them at night in your dreams, and even experience a visual materialization of your loved one's spirit, all of which is considered part of a normal adaptation process.[11]

In his book *The Soul in Grief*, Robert Romanyshyn describes this state of liminality quite poignantly following the sudden death of his wife:

> . . . you inhabit a nether world between sleep and wakefulness, a place where you are neither in a dream nor fully in the world. You dwell in a moment which is neither night nor day, a twilight world of shadows and light, a world whose darkness is more than the darkest night and whose light is less than the cloudiest of days.[12]

During quiet moments alone, you may see hallucinogenic images of your loved one bathed in light, or hear him or her call out to you. These images can be very frightening when they come upon you suddenly and unexpectedly, as they often do. A man whose wife died in his arms of a sudden stroke, had such a vision while sleeping:

I see Cheryl directly in front of me from the waist up. She has very blond, almost golden hair and is wearing an aqua-colored shirt. At first, I don't recognize her, but then I do and am very, very frightened so that I wake myself up. Drenched in sweat and heart racing, I cry deeply because I now realize that it was she and I am ashamed that I was so frightened. She might think that I would never want to see her and that I made her go away.

A mother whose son was tragically killed while on a business trip went to the room where his body was found and experienced his energy "in the form of lights, like little fireflies that filled the room." Back at home several weeks later, she clairvoyantly heard him say: "Wow! I've turned into something really big!" "I didn't hear his voice," she says, "but knew he was speaking to me. I believe it meant that he had transcended his physical body and had become pure energy—he had expanded enormously and was very excited about it."

The time span of this phase may be as short as a month or two, or it may continue on and off for a year, or even longer with extremely tragic deaths. As with all phases, its length and intensity depends on the closeness of the relationship and its complexity at the time of death. Western society anticipates that a month or two should be enough time to recover from a sudden loss and that it is best to return to work and everyday life by then. In many other cultures, however, the bereaved are allowed a year or longer to adjust, giving them and the soul of the departed the time for a smooth transition from a life shared to one apart. These cultures recognize and acknowledge the state of liminality and don't expect major transitions to occur as suddenly as we do in Western society.

Dreams during this liminal phase tend to be characteristic of transliminal dreams (see above). While in this state, you feel as if you have become one with death and that death has almost fully absorbed your consciousness. Dream images and symbols tend to be highly archetypal and can easily be associated with the death and funerary rites of ancient times. Your dream ego may encounter disembodied spirits, participate in death rites, and be faced with the starkness of death in a very personal way.

Significant dream themes are often encountered during this phase, all of which connect you symbolically and psychically with the world of the dead. The death tunnel and bridal chamber commonly seen in near-death experiences may be one of the first of these images to appear. You may encounter a passageway as a tunnel, either in the earth or on another dimension of reality; you may be alone or with the deceased; you may enter a chamber that contains a radiant bright light. Raymond Moody, in his research on near-death experiences, has heard the death tunnel and chamber described as "a cave, a well, a trough, an enclosure, a tunnel, a funnel, a vacuum, a void, a sewer, a valley, and a cylinder."[13] Such tunnel- and cave-like images are universally viewed as the transitional state of death and are portrayed as such in the architecture of Egyptian tombs. It is believed that these passageways connect the physical with the spiritual or transcendent world. In the tombs, the tunnel drops into a chamber below the earth, believed by the Egyptians, and the Greeks as well, to be the bridal chamber or earth womb where the dead await rebirth.

Von Franz states that this tunnel motif "anticipates the course of death." Its representation in your psyche is an archetypal connection between the worlds of the living and the dead.[14] When dreaming, you may encounter that other realm of consciousness and be shown something new about the transitional state of death that you did not know before. Tunnel dreams often leave you with a sense of peace and intentionality about the events that have transpired in your life, unless you have difficulty getting into the tunnel.

Dismembered Osiris from ancient Egypt may also appear early in the dreams of the bereaved and especially during moments of deep emotional pain. In the Egyptian *Book of the Dead*, it is said that every person becomes Osiris, the god of resurrection, at the moment of death. Osiris is the deity of Egyptian afterlife, a god who appears more often than any other in their ancient *Pyramid Texts*. To those who acknowledge the archetypal level of the collective unconscious, it is not surprising that Osiris is so prominent in the dreams of the bereaved. He is an inherited energy form, an archetype from those ancient times that is a part of your soul even today. Osiris is believed to have been the first divinely born king of Egypt, who suffered a profoundly tragic death. In his mythical story, he is killed by his jealous brother, Seth, who smothers him in a lead box and severs him into thirteen pieces. Isis, Osiris' sister-wife and goddess of great power in her own right, searches for and collects his body parts, then reassembles them. Osiris eventually returns to life, but is believed to remain in the underworld, where he "rules as King of Eternity and supreme judge of the dead."[15]

Osiris often appears in dreams as a dismembered body of a loved one. The parts may or may not be in a case or chest; they may be treated in ritual fashion; they may resurrect from the earthly plane in a burst of transcendent sparkles. The appearance of Osiris in dreams suggests the resurrection of physical matter into transcendent form, a representation of the continuation of the life of the soul.[16]

The recycling and blooming of trees, fields of flowers, and other plant life also occur early in bereavement dreams. Plant life and its cyclical nature recall resurrection, everlasting life, and the promise of a continued existence. Plants regain life from dead, inorganic matter, and have a life-death nature.

In many religious traditions, flowers and plants are placed on caskets and graves as a symbol of this everlasting cycle of life and death. In the dreams of the bereaved, flowers may appear at special places associated with a lost love, or may suddenly appear as a gift from an unknown place. Often, such profound bursts of color and life leave you with a sense of peace and a deep, unexplainable knowing that life does continue beyond the darkness of the grave.

Seeking, Rescuing, and Visiting

A longing for your departed loved one may be expressed in your dreams through lengthy searches, coupled with attempts to rescue him or her from their death. You may call out for a visit in whatever way is possible, and may ritualize your longing in an outer ceremony familiar to you. Such expressions of love and grief prepare the way for your loved one to meet with you when the time is right.

It is not unusual for there to be a period of time immediately following a death when there is a complete absence of your departed love in your dreams. In some cases, the departed may be unavailable during that period. In all of the dream series in this book, visitations did not occur until several months after the death. This is not always the case, but does appear to be a pattern. Robert Crookall, specialist in psychic research, stated in his book *"Dreams" of High Significance* that the newly deceased "must have the opportunity of that emotional review of their past lives that obviously corresponds to the Judgment of all religions. It is best that this important series of experiences should proceed undisturbed by calls from mortals."[17] He continues:

> The possibility of contact with dead loved ones will be increased if the habit of out-going, helpful, loving and understanding activities is formed. It is good practice, before going out in sleep to offer to give any practical help. When these two conditions are fulfilled, significant dreams of the dead are nearly facilitated.[18]

Tibetan Sogyal Rinpoche observes that:

> The most powerful time to do spiritual practice for someone who has died is during the forty-nine days of the bardo of becoming, placing special emphasis on the first twenty-one days. It is during

these first three weeks that the dead have a stronger link with this life, which makes them more accessible to our help.[19]

Dreams during this period include attempts by your dream ego to rescue the departed loved one, images or sightings of your loved one living elsewhere even though you know she or he is dead, pleas for a visit, and, as in the previous phase, archetypal images of death. Visitation dreams begin now, if they have not already, and may continue for several months. Generally, the first visitation comes suddenly and quite unexpectedly. You are surprised and emotionally elated to be having this time together. Physical holding and lovemaking may take place, especially if it was part of the relationship prior to the death. Such contacts are also considered part of the healing process. These moments are intensely sensuous and may be experienced as if they were indeed happening. There may be only one or two of these visits, or they may continue on and off for several months, or even longer if bereavement becomes complicated.

These visitations serve a meaningful purpose for the bereaved as well as the deceased. Talks tend to revolve around the painful separation process, issues of grief and unfinished business, and how your loved one is experiencing the afterlife. The deceased may be tremendously happy and look much healthier than before death, especially if the death was caused by an illness. Occasionally, however, he or she may appear as ill and unhappy as they did before death. It is at these times that your loved one needs your prayers the most. These visitations are a gift to you and you must acknowledge and engage in them, if you can, with all of your heart and soul. It is an opportunity for you to say your last good-byes, to help each other continue in your separate journeys, and to realize that your loved one's essence lives on in your soul in spite of its absence in your everyday life.

Separation and Parting

Unfortunately, your dream visitations cannot continue indefinitely. Your loved one's presence in your dreams slowly decreases, or she or he may become distracted by something or someone else in your dreams. You may have difficulty meeting because barriers arise, some of which are created by the very one you love. Sometimes the departed clearly says "I have to go on," and develops a relationship with previously deceased persons or archetypal images of gods and goddesses. You may observe their union with the universe in what is known as a "death wedding" or "sacred marriage." Such a marriage is a "union of the soul with the universe, with the *anima mundi* (Mother World) in the womb of nature," a marriage with the cosmic dimension.[20] Jung experienced this sacred marriage as a mystical journey between life and death while in a near-death state following his first heart attack:

> . . . I was Rabbi Simon ben Jochai, whose wedding in the afterlife was being celebrated. It was the mystic marriage as it appears in the Cabbalistic tradition . . . I do not know exactly what part I played in it. At bottom, it was I myself: I was the marriage. And my beatitude was that of a blissful wedding.[21]

Resurrection of the soul after death is a *coniunctio*, "a coming together of the white (dove) and the black (Arvin), the latter being the spirit that dwells in the tombstone."[22] In rural Greece, the funeral process is a celebration of this very union. It involves several stages, from the original burial soon after death, to a second burial years later. In the second burial, the remains of the deceased are recovered, ritually treated, and stored permanently in a community grave. The remains are joined with the ancestors of the community—symbolically, with the universal soul. If the death was of an unmarried child, the analogy becomes even clearer, as the funeral is actually celebrated as a wedding. In many areas of Greece, a young, unmarried person is buried dressed in wedding clothes, and parts of a young woman's dowry are buried with her in her coffin.[23]

The mother who lost her fourteen-year-old daughter in a car accident dreamed:

Michelle has been killed in a plane accident and I have come to claim her belongings. I look in a scrapbook she was compiling and find an invitation to her future wedding. I think "My Michelle was organized. She already has her wedding invitation filed away here."

Several months later, she dreamed:

We are organizing Michelle's funeral, but it also seems to be her wedding. Most of the women are dressed either in black or in white. Suddenly, I realize that this is, indeed, Michelle's funeral and that I am saying goodbye forever to my dearest daughter.

It is meant for the departed to go forward in his or her soul's journey rather than cling to or feel responsible for your emotional work here on Earth. Sogyal Rinpoche claims that, at first, the departed have a strong connection to the life they leave behind, but, not long after, their "future life slowly takes shape and becomes the dominant influence." If they remain attached to the material world through a dependent relationship with those left behind, or are unable themselves to progress in their soul's journey, they may remain as a non-entity in ghostly form.[24] In *Guidance from Beyond*, Kate Wingfield clearly states: "It would hinder a Soul from progressing on the other side if it were able continually to come back and speak with those it left behind."[25]

Now the work of releasing the bond begins. Your dreams may contain painful memories of a life you shared together, now gone. Fantasies and day-dreams may preoccupy your daily movements. Feelings of sadness, regrets, guilt, and pleasure over what you had come to you often, and you enter the darkness of your soul's longing for what you have lost.

Emotional Chaos

Feelings of abandonment strike hard in this phase, which may begin weeks after the death or many months later, and may last for years. How you expe-rience your grief and dreams is uniquely individual. No one person's experi-ence is the same as another's. A deep, gnawing sadness may permeate your everyday life, or you may be filled with profound guilt and self-blame over things not done or said, or about unfortunate circumstances surrounding the death. Anger and fury may erupt, especially if a loved one was taken before his or her time or the death was sudden and unexpected. When this is the case, the death can be more difficult to assimilate and may result in a stag-nant state of chronic yearning and longing. Your dreams portray such emo-tional chaos in images that can be very disturbing to your waking ego.

Guilt filled my unconscious when I entered the phase of emotional chaos five months after my son's death. It began with a dream:

I see Michael at home with his friends, but don't respond to him, "since I see him all the time anyway." Suddenly, I realize I should have talked to him when I had the chance because "he is going to die." I return quickly, but too late; then agonize over having missed my last moments with him. Later, in another dream, I say: "I want to talk to him but can't—it seems as if there's a glass between us. I can see his sadness and despondency but can't communicate with him."

Guilt for not being available to my son when he was with me, coupled with feelings of inadequacy as the mother of an adolescent boy, kept me from connecting with him. Painful regrets pervaded my nightly dreams for close to a year, and then finally, a resolution began to appear. When you remain connected to the soul dimension of your dreams, the place at which you are able to relate to your departed loved one, resolution can and often does take place.

During this phase of emotional chaos, dreams often come forth in nightmarish images of death and dying, with attempts to survive a dark and life-threatening storm. A mother who lost her son in a homicidal death dreams:

I am fighting black sails in a dark night storm. The wind is strong and rain is hard. All I can do is battle the sails.

Again she dreams:

I'm lying on the ground with many dead bodies—all killed by the gang. We are wrapped together in white cloth that is tied around with rope. I have to pretend I am dead so I won't be killed too—can hardly breathe and am terrified that I will be noticed and shot.

Another mother dreams:

I see a tiny girl behind the door of the cupboard. She is scared, naked, malnourished, and has a poor color. She wants to come out but is too frightened. Then, I finally convince her to come out. She is mute, cannot talk, and looks imploringly into the eyes of the man and spells out a word on his lower thigh—"H.E.L.P."

It is now when you feel as though God has forsaken you and you must fight the unbearable darkness and reality of death alone. You become engaged with the archetype of the Dark Night Storm (also known as the Night Sea Journey), an active and violent energy that surrounds you with the emotional eruption of deep suffering. St. John of the Cross states:

> . . . no means or remedy is of any service or profit for the relief of its affliction; the more so because the soul is as powerless in this case as one who has been imprisoned in a dark dungeon, and is bound hand and foot, and can neither move nor see, nor feel any favour whether from above or from below, until the spirit is humbled, softened and purified . . .[26]

Jung claims: "Those black waters of death are the water of life, for death with its cold embrace is the maternal womb, just as the sea devours the sun but brings it forth again."[27] He conceives of this state as a positive one, in which "the soul learns to commune with God with more respect and more courtesy, such as a soul must ever observe in converse with the most high."[28] Von Franz believes that the less familiar one is with the dark side of God, the greater will be her or his negative experience of death.[29]

Often in these dreams, your psychic condition becomes synonymous with death, showing clearly how much the survival of your ego is at the mercy of forces beyond your control. Your dreams become riddled with scenes of killings and tragedies as you stand by helplessly observing the death of, not only the one you've lost, but also those who are still alive. You may panic that you will lose another loved one, or you may experience your own death and pass through the death tunnel to meet with the bright light on the other side. Such dreams are confusing and terribly frightening, but what you must realize is that, when your psyche encounters such powerful emotions as the Dark Night, you are facing the death of who or what you once were. Such death images in dreams are not physical deaths, but the transformation of your emotional and ego-driven self. They are a positive synthesis of the bereavement process.

In the alchemical process of transformation, darkness and suffering are the *negredo*, or blackness, that corresponds to the unknown shadow element, or chaos, of the unconscious. Through your conscious effort to enter this blackness, with its intense pain and suffering, you transform it and the unconsciousness it represents into illumination, the *albedo*, or white element of the transformation process.

St. John of the Cross states:

> The first and principal benefit which the soul derives from this arid and dark night of contemplation is the knowledge of its own self and its own misery. . . . In this dark night the word of the prophet is fulfilled: "Thy light shall shine in the darkness" (Is. 58:10). . . . And thus we see clearly that from this arid night comes first of all self-knowledge, and this in turn is the foundation from which arises the knowledge of God. This is why St. Augustine said to God: "Let me know myself, oh Lord, and I shall know Thee" (Soliloq., Chap. 2) . . . And from this wonderful spiritual sobriety follow further great benefits; for, when the desires are subjugated

and silenced, the soul lives in spiritual tranquility and in peace. . . . and the soul can say: "My house was at last in deepest rest."[30]

Internalization and Regeneration

During this phase of bereavement, the emotional intensity naturally decreases and, generally speaking, a lengthy period of years has passed since the loss. There is a final acceptance of the death. Most likely, you have developed new life patterns without your loved one, although there may be occasional eruptions of sadness and a painful longing during anniversaries and significant periods in the relationship. Emotional chaos and the dark night experience have passed and your loved one in your dreams tends now to represent an aspect of your subjective self rather than the objective presence she or he was shortly after death. Kast terms this phase, "New Relationship to Oneself and the World," which describes this phase positively with your newfound path in life following the darkness of deep suffering. She claims that the precondition for this phase is that "the deceased has become an inner figure" who also evolves in your dreams, or the relationship that you had together now becomes part of your potential in life.[31] Common themes of this include the birthing of babies with superior qualities, interactions with your departed loved one at various ages and stages of life, the supportive presence of same-sex characters who are images of your positive shadow aspects, and guidance from the opposite sex that shows you places previously unknown to you.

Your loved one may also become a spirit guide who leads you into the underworld or the transcendent dimension, or may give you supportive advice during times of difficulty and crises in your life. In her study of more than 1,500 dreams following the loss of a loved one, Dierdre Barrett found that 23 percent contained advice offered by the departed. Many of these dreams offer helpful advice or warn about life-threatening issues.[32] Death researcher Joel Martin sees deep value in such after-death communications and guidance, stating: "There is no greater, more binding love than that between parent and child [lover and spouse], and through direct after-death communications, we know that death does not diminish or break this bond."[33]

Relapses also occur during this phase. They may surprise you when they come, because you are generally now content and involved with life. Even an instant of loss, whether it is positive or negative, can result in sadness and depression as you remember that your loved one is no longer with you. These periods of depression tend not to be quite as strong or pervasive as they were earlier, however. Kast views these episodes as "opportunities to assimilate loss experiences in general and in particular the one great loss."[34]

I was taken by a long period of depression eighteen months after Michael's death, upon completing my two-year Masters program and receiving my long-sought degree. "Why," I wondered, "would I be feeling so sad at a time like this?" Then I had the following dream:

The world is coming to an end. I am in school and everyone leaves. I quit tending to my appearance and wear an old gray sweatshirt and cry a lot. I want to spend time with Ed and Cora before the world ends. There is an announcement at school that everyone should go home. I do and feel that Michael is around somewhere—I see his drawings and personal things, and sense that there is a way to contact him. I know he is doing well and feel pride for what he has accomplished.

This is a significant dream because it not only addresses the reason behind my depression, but also reveals a way beyond it. By going home in solitude to the place of my true Self, I will see how much I have given to the budding potential of Michael within me. Every loss I experienced in my life, even my lost childhood, came to be represented in my dreams as an image of Michael. Was this my soul's way of reminding me that all losses come to the same place? It is certainly true that a loss of any kind is a death of a part of oneself. Following this, can it not also be true that the deepest and most profound losses within us are symbolized by the greatest loss in our lives?

Complications within the bereavement process or unfinished business in the relationship may occasionally appear in your dreams in various ways, unless you are able to resolve them during the first years following the death. Full resolution by this time tends not to be the pattern, however. All you can do following a tragic loss is to work through your overwhelming emotional chaos and develop a new life pattern without your loved one. Generally, this takes years to do.

Dream images of being stuck in the bereavement process or in the relationship are revealed in many ways during the phase of regeneration. Some of these images include:

- An unburied corpse—an indication that there is a denial of the death or that mourning is not complete;

- A longing for and inability to connect with your loved one because unfinished business and guilt keeps the union from happening;
- Images of disfigurement or disability that evolve from a distorted view of the relationship that was shared together.

Because the world of your dreams is so individually unique and rich in symbolic imagery and metaphor, there are more images than can possibly be presented here that can be associated with a problem or complex. What's important is your willingness to work with the images that don't seem quite right, courage to explore areas that are deeply painful, and the strength to go beyond your ingrained belief system. In short, you must have the courage to confront your shadow. Generally, such work requires guidance and support in an analytic container—or at least you must have some knowledge or awareness of the soul's journey, coupled with an ego strong enough to confront such painful material alone.

Many people remain in the phase of regeneration for the remainder of their lives and are able to cope adequately in their day-to-day activities and routines. Grief may come to them from time to time if it has not been fully resolved, or they may have completed all they can with the loss, short of internalizing their loved one as a positive aspect of their being.

Reunion / Renewal

Decades may pass with memories of your loved one tucked neatly in a special part of your heart, occasionally reminding you of the influence he or she had in your life. These memories may appear in your dreams as subjective aspects of yourself, or they may not appear at all. You may think that they are long gone, until suddenly one night, you find yourself visiting with your loved one in a dream as if they had never left. Most likely, the visitation occurs when a new event is about to occur. It may be something of which you are conscious, or it may be the approaching death, possibly beyond your awareness, of someone very close.

In his *Memories, Dreams, Reflections*, Carl Jung describes a sudden visitation from his deceased father who had not been in his dreams for twenty-six years. The dream came to him four months before his mother's death. Jung says that it appeared as if his father "had returned from a distant journey."

His presence was "refreshed" and he did not have that air of authority that Jung remembered of him when he was alive. Deeply excited about this visit from his long-lost father, Jung was preparing to share life and death experiences with him. He quickly realized, however, that this was not the purpose of the visit. His father seemed preoccupied, as if wanting something from his son, which he communicated once Jung's enthusiasm settled down. The purpose of his visit, he said, was to seek his son's psychological services for "marital psychology." Then Jung woke up. He says: "I could not properly understand the dream, for it never occurred to me that it might refer to my mother's death. I realized that only when she died suddenly [four months later] in January 1923."[35]

Jung pondered his visitation dream at length and came to the conclusion that the dream had more to do with his father than himself. Since his father's wife was soon to be "passing over" and perhaps resuming their relationship, he "wished to ask a psychologist about the newest insights and information on marital problems." According to Jung, their earthly marriage had been filled with "trials and difficulties." This dream is significant because, as Jung states: "Evidently [his father] had acquired no better understanding in his timeless state and therefore had to appeal to someone among the living who, enjoying the benefits of changed times, might have a fresh approach to the whole thing."[36]

Jung had another experience of this kind in a dream of his wife, Emma, a year after her death. In the dream, they were together in Provence, France, while she was working on her studies of the Grail myth, which she did not complete before her death. Jung attempted to interpret his dream on the subjective level as his anima, but it produced nothing for him that he did not already know. He concluded that she was continuing this very important work after death. "That my wife was continuing after death to work on her further spiritual development—however that may be conceived—struck me as meaningful and held a measure of reassurance for me," he said.[37]

Jung's dreams suggest that our departed loved ones continue their soul's journey even after death. Jung and von Franz have both emphasized that "the unconscious psyche pays very little attention to the abrupt end of bodily life and behaves as if the psychic life of the individual, that is, the individuation process, will simply continue." Von Franz states: "The unconscious *believes* quite obviously in a life after death."[38] While writing his *Septem Sermones ad*

Mortuos, Jung sensed he was in communication with spirits of the deceased, who he said, "addressed crucial questions to me. They came—so they said— 'back from Jerusalem, where they found not what they sought'."[39] Christian teachings intimate that, once deceased, we become "possessors of great knowledge." According to Jung's experience and the dreams of the bereaved, however, this does not appear to be the case. "Apparently . . . , the souls of the dead 'know' only what they knew at the moment of death, and nothing beyond that. Hence their endeavor to penetrate into life in order to share in the knowledge of men."[40]

Ten years after my son's death, I found myself suddenly trying to connect with him in a dream. While delving into an archetypal analysis of the dreams I had following Michael's death for my analytic thesis, this highly emotional moment came to me quite suddenly.

Michael is back as if he had never died. I have been involved at a school and he is now college age, but rather than go to school, he hangs out in the house of his best friend. They appear to have an open drug policy there. Feeling worried about Michael, I telephone to talk to him, but he doesn't want to speak to me. I see many boys his age smoking various dried weeds that are stored in jars lined up on a shelf. I get angry and go into the bathroom to sit on the pot and think. As I sit there, I see a vague image of a young man smoking behind the shower curtain as he stares out an open window. I think about this longer and become aware of the fact that he is my son who is trapped there and can't get out because I'm in his way.

There is no doubt that this is a reunion dream, and an especially painful one at that. It was very difficult for me to avoid seeing how bad our relationship had been at the time of Michael's death, and that I was deceiving myself about the idealized image I had of us together. Two significant realities are evident here. I had not resolved the angry feelings I had toward Michael when he died, and Michael had not grown beyond his difficulties since his death. In the dream, he is caught in what appears to be a state of limbo as he smokes psychedelics and stares out an open window. Was it my lack of consciousness about our relationship that kept him in this no-man's land? I am the one attempting to make contact in the dream, so it appears that, if anything is worked through, it will have to be up to me. It was clear that Michael was not in the place to act, nor to engage with me. The outcome of this dream is discussed in the presentation of my bereavement dream series in the next chapter. What is important here is that Michael's painful situation was shown to me at a time when I was open to seeing the difficulties we had together. These difficulties kept me not only from doing the work I needed to do, but also kept Michael's soul in what appeared to be a limbo-like place.

The Tibetans believe that the departed can suffer as much emotional pain in the afterlife as we do here on Earth, and that our prayers and rituals can help them through their pain and suffering. Sogyal Rinpoche states: "The radiant power and warmth of the compassionate heart can reach out to help in all states and all realms."[41] When you use your dreams as a guiding source and work with them as directly and as honestly as you can, not only do you grow emotionally and spiritually, but it appears that your departed loved ones grow as well. Such work can result in major transformations in your unconscious that are often symbolized in dreams as your loved one's resurrection from the confinement of death. These "rising from the grave" motifs may represent a turning point in your bereavement or the awakening of a dead part of yourself. They may represent a resolution of your relationship with your departed loved one, as well as their growth and recovery in the world of the beyond. Kast claims that, when you have a resurrection dream, it marks the ending of a phase of mourning and the beginning of a new relationship with the deceased. It is the beginning of a life renewed and "marks a turning point in the experience with death."[42] You become one with death, experience it, and, through that experience, are reborn in a new way. It is a rising of a dead part within you represented as an image of the one whom you've loved and lost. It may also be a renewed vitality of your loved one who has passed over.

My husband had such a dream while in analysis for a period out of a need to save our relationship. About a year into his inner work, he dreamed:

We have to move Michael's body from an above-ground container and I have to follow a procedure for it to be opened. Geri is with me and a worker of some kind. I write the procedure down in a notebook. The worker removes the cover from the container and Michael's nude body is exposed. We observe him lying there and notice that an expression appears on his face. He starts to move his upper body, slowly sits up in the casket and gets out. We are ecstatic that he is alive and discuss how he should come home with us. In the end, I lead the way in my truck and Michael drives Geri in the car behind me.

This dream is important because in it, Ed was involved in the resurrection process. He used a notebook (his dream journal?) to record the procedure and, from that, the return to life unfolded. Everyone celebrates the occasion and Michael, the newly resurrected aspect of Ed, becomes a part of our relationship. Ed's self-realization is deeply connected to his son. I can only speculate what may have helped Michael's soul through Ed's inner work, but, from all indications, it may very well have been something positive.

Transcendence and Transformation

There is no doubt that the sudden loss of a loved one by death impels you to question the meaning of your existence and challenges your belief in God. Powerful dreams revealing the sacred dimension from which you feel isolated may arise to compensate for this struggle and to show you the answers that you seek. These dreams bring the sacred back into your life and guide you to ever-deepening dimensions of the psyche, until you may find yourself face-to-face with the essence of your soul.

Such dreams are dreams of transcendence, and they come at any time in the bereavement process. One young mother had a transcendent-like dream only eight days after her son's death.

I am in a large room with many women—women of all nations in their native dress: black women in African dress, Oriental women in Mandarin clothes, etc. I am wearing a long, red dress with gold embroidered trim and a gold belt with a sash around my hips. I am barefooted, waist length hair (as now) and braids down the front. Drums begin a beat. We are all happy and begin to dance, waving our arms and smiling. We dance to the beat and begin to rub our bellies. I hear a gentle female voice saying: "This is to celebrate your motherhood!"

The woman says: "To have this profound dream so soon after my son's death left all of my senses 'tuned in' so to speak. I knew more would be coming. The words 'this is to celebrate your motherhood' have stuck to me to this day."

Transcendence is a heightened state of functioning that goes beyond ordinary conscious reality. At these intense moments, you may see visions and have feelings of overwhelming joy and bliss that project a sense of meaning and purpose into your existence. Such moments may come upon you in your dreams or in your waking life. They are highly compensatory to your suffering and most certainly show you another reality beyond that suffering.

Spontaneous periods of transcendence are not rare experiences. Studies show that from 50 to 85 percent of Americans have experienced them.[43] Natural conditions that are conducive to such experiences include focusing your consciousness on thoughts of reverie, fantasy, or daydreaming; experiencing a new and unusually demanding activity and environment, such as mountain climbing and nature retreats; living in a harshly deprived and frustrating situation; working from your creative depth; experiencing depression or deep physical or emotional pain and anguish; and the state of dreaming. Romanyshyn shares his painful experience over the death of his beloved wife in his book, *The Soul in Grief.* He describes how he coped by consciously entering states of reverie on natural and spiritual images that held meaning for him. He says:

> Now, when I can allow myself to be embraced by these occasions, when I can let myself sink in reverie below the busyness of my mind, when I can honor how the death of my wife opened my soul, I am also honoring her in sadness and in joy. In these moments, I marvel at the power of grief to open the soul to the hidden and forgotten radiance of beauty in the world.[44]

Such heightened states of awareness may come to you spontaneously and quite unexpectedly when you are sleeping, or during the day when you are listening to music that touches your soul. They may come during more structured occasions, as in religious ceremonies and rituals, or long periods of introversion and meditation. And not uncommonly, they may come to you when you are on the threshold of dying. Seldom can heightened states be induced consciously, unless you engage in psychedelics or structured physical deprivations, as in holotropic breath work. When the moment hits you, you are suddenly struck with a feeling of profound bliss, ecstasy, and euphoria, and may cry deeply over what has come over you. You may feel a powerful oneness with the universe and feel the radiance of God's hand upon you. Afterward, you may sense that you have a new relationship with the divine—an intimacy and connection that wasn't felt before—and have suddenly gained a new perception of the meaning of life. Such wonderful moments of transcendence may last for only a few minutes, but their effect on your thoughts and emotions can continue for days or even weeks afterward. Experiencing the transcendent is known to result in significant and permanent changes in your personality. The sudden and premature death of a loved one engages you intimately with death and the underworld and brings you closer to the divine. When you are given such a life experience, you are never the same again.

The morning after I had a very emotional conversation about Michael with his friend, David, I awoke in ecstasy following a dream vision of fireworks and glittery, hand-held spirals twirling in the wind, all to the tune of the theme song from *Terms of Endearment*. Only two weeks after my son's death, I wrote in my journal: "I feel ecstatic, like I have accomplished something wonderful and I am in celebration of it." The emotions I felt following this profound dream were a far cry from the emotions I had felt the night before. "How strange" I thought, "to be feeling this way now when I have just lost my son." The dream I had was a vision dream that reflected the numinous quality of the wind of God and the radiant circles of the soul image. It revealed to me the oneness that we all share when we commune through the universal reality of life, death, and loss. I knew that something profound had been constellated within my soul, brought on by the conversation with my son's friend. Through the music, *Terms of Endearment*, it affirmed the special relationship I had with Michael, in spite of our many conflicts.

Encountering the transpersonal dimension is a personal encounter with your soul. It is a coming together of your ego awareness with the dimension of your psyche referred to as the Self. Such a union results in what Jung calls the "transcendent function," a joining of the opposites within you. It not only provides you with a temporary respite from the deep pain you are experiencing, but reveals an order of things beyond your conscious reality. The spaceless and timeless dimension of the divine celebrates death and shows your ego self that it is not the end to the person who appears to have been taken from you. We all "have the capacity to transcend our ordinary existence and to feel in touch with the infinite."[45] We all have it in us to experience the love of God and, through our suffering, to become one with Him.

Bereavement dreams come and go for many decades after you have suffered the loss of a loved one. As you will see in the dream stories to come, they clearly have a pattern and intentionality to them. The dream process is not a linear one, but is experienced as a spiral, with one dream phase seeming to end, to return later with an image or situation that you weren't prepared to see before. One phase does not complete before another begins; rather they overlap, one upon another. As time passes, your bereavement dreams become further and further apart, until they end, and you feel the presence of your loved one always with you. Sometimes, a closure dream may come to you—a dream visit in which you sit with your loved one or a person of divine qualities to share a profound moment together. It is at these times—when you know you have come into your own and that, through your profound suffering, you have come to know death and the divine—that the radiance of death is revealed to you.

Part Two

EXPERIENCING
DEATH

chapter four

FROM DISMEMBERMENT TO UNION—MY STORY

. . . a woman who held a babe against her bosom said, Speak to us of Children.
And he said: Your children are not your children.
They are the sons and daughters of Life's longing for itself.
They come through you but not from you,
And though they are with you yet they belong not to you.
You may give them your love but not your thoughts,
For they have their own thoughts.
You may house their bodies but not their souls,
For their souls dwell in the house of tomorrow, which you cannot visit, not even in your dreams.
You may strive to be like them, but seek not to make them like you.
For life goes not backward nor tarries with yesterday.

—KAHLIL GIBRAN, *The Prophet*

Michael, my only son and first-born child, was a happy, loving boy until his diagnosed "educational disability" and my need to have him improve his school performance drove a wedge between us. This did not become a serious problem, however, until he turned fourteen and entered the competitive world of high school where peer pressure, increased hormonal activity, and my preoccupied life in search of a career quickly amplified it. In a short time, he suddenly became his "own person," so that my attempts to be an influence in his life were met with a normal

young man's determination to fight off "the devouring mother." One morning following another of our angry episodes, I had an intensely emotional and
sensuous dream that affected me deeply. The dream was potently charged with
archetypal images of death that were beyond my comprehension at the time.
Although obvious to me now, I was unable to understand its prophetic message. This is what I dreamed:

*I am making arrangements to buy something related to tennis and do it in a forceful way. Then
one night, Ed, Cora, Michael, and I are sleeping in an apartment high up in a tall building. I
hear dogs howling below in the dark night. Several men climb a ladder and enter our apartment
through a window. I hear Michael run out of his room to see who it is. I know they are going
to hurt us and am afraid for my son. One of the men strikes Michael on the back of the head
with a tennis racket and kills him; another comes through my window and hurts me as well,
but not fatally. I scream at the intruder and cry so hard I can't get the words out.*

*In the morning, a group of young boys clean up the mess. I cry hard and ask if some-
thing can be done to change this, but nothing I say works. Suddenly Ed, Cora, and I are at a
church attending Michael's funeral. Boys his age are reading in ritual fashion. I cry very hard
and ask a male presence if it really has to happen.*

"Is he really dead?"

"Yes, he's dead."

*In anguish, I plead for a better outcome: "Does it have to happen? Is it really the end?
He would have been such a nice young man."*

*I am awakened from my sleep by the primitive sound of a rattle, record my dream, and
return to a twilight state. As I doze, I feel the body of a large, fat snake wrapped around my
neck. I am more intrigued by its presence than afraid of it. The snake feels unusually warm
and soothing for such an experience.*

Immediately following this dream, my first conscious thought is that I am
experiencing the agony of losing my little boy, that his growing up feels like a
death to me. "Yes, it really has to happen," I am told. Generally, death dreams
are not of an actual forewarned event; rather they represent the death of a relationship or a subjective aspect of the psyche.[1] I know now, however, that my
dream was a prophetic one, with the archetypes of death portrayed clearly and
strongly in it. The prophecy had an ominous quality, as I tried futilely to
change what had already been put into motion. It appears that the dream was
sent to prepare me for what was to come eighteen months later; or it could
have been a warning to me that my focus on achievement would lead to this.

A forewarned feeling or dream of some future disaster or death is not a rare occurrence. In Aniela Jaffé's research on apparitions and precognition phenomena, she finds that a majority of the cases sent to her contained instances of precognition, some of which helped save the dreamer from an impending disaster and others about which the dreamer could do nothing. Such instances can be "regarded as the signs or heralds of a higher power to which man has to submit" she says.[2] Tibetan medical texts contain warning signs of impending doom, such as dreams that foretell a death within days or years of the event. Sogyal Rinpoche claims: "Their purpose is to forewarn a person that his or her life is in danger, and to alert the person to using practices that lengthen life, before these obstacles occur."[3]

The first words in my dream are: "I am making arrangements to buy something related to tennis." At the time, my association with tennis was: "there must be something more to life than just tennis"—thoughts I had at a time when I felt disillusioned about the meaninglessness and lack of spiritual significance in my life. Tennis is also a competitive sport and, in the dream, I am being forceful about it. Was my forcefulness destroying the relationship I had with my son? I was certainly driving him away from me so forcefully that I was out of touch with the fate that appeared to be ordained.

"We are sleeping in an apartment high up in a tall building," far from the groundedness of the Earth. "I hear dogs howling below in the dark." Dogs guard the realm between physical life and the underworld. In ancient myths and legends of Europe, the dog represents the preying and devouring aspects of death, as well as a healing and protecting escort into the underworld. In my dream, the dogs howl and a burglar breaks into our safe, isolated haven. Two unexpected death elements break into my secluded place high above the Earth and create havoc in my life. My son is the family volunteer who courageously faces them, and he is the one struck dead. As in real life, he is killed by a head injury.

The dream becomes ritualistic at this point, as young men clean up and read at his funeral. His death is a "coming of age" to the young men who are his friends. Its reality strikes them harshly and deeply. In the church, I am in profound, agonizing grief as I encounter the archetype of death and see clearly its reality. I struggle to change the bargain I made for a life with spiritual meaning, to no avail. What this bargain may be is beyond my comprehension. I wonder, perhaps, if it is something I created before this lifetime—a karmic debt? I am awakened from the dream by a rattle, which seems strangely similar to a *sistrum*, an ancient instrument of percussion from the Egyptian era. It has an archaic quality to it. The sistrum, a metal rattle with an oval frame, was used by the Egyptians to ward off sleep and, therefore, psychological death.[4]

After I awaken from the dream and return to a pre-sleep state, I feel a healing snake gently wrapped around my neck, as if to warm and soothe me. The snake, one of the most spiritual of all creatures, has many meanings, but primarily it represents a primeval, cosmic force. It expresses a numinous quality that underlies the mystery of death. According to Greek myths, the image of the snake intensifies the horror aspect of death and is strongly healing.[5]

The snake is the animal of Aesculapius, the god of ancient Greece who heals mortal men. The snake, and also the dog, are two intimate attributes of Aesculapius—he often becomes one or the other during times of healing. During the Aesculapian era, the sick and ailing went to Epidaurus, his famous healing temple, and slept in the innermost chamber of the sanctuary. Their sleep time was called an incubation; their healing came about through a dream encounter with the god himself. Often, he appeared in the image of a dog or a snake who, occasionally, touched the affected part of the incubant's body to produce the healing.[6]

My prophetic dream appears to be a preparation for what was to come. It seemed to be revealing that, even though I would suffer the catastrophic loss of my son, I would be cared for and healed by the archetypes of the soul. The healing revealed itself in the form of a snake. Aesculapius was the wound and also the remedy: "He who has wounded also heals."[7] The snake added a sacred dimension to the catastrophe that was to come, and it was important for me to be aware of this.

Carl Meier claims that the ancient themes of incubation as a source of healing are still very much alive in our psyches today. I experienced it strongly through the howling of the dogs and the feeling of the snake wrapped gently around my neck. When I had this dream twenty years ago, I knew little about the spiritual dimension of the psyche, or of archetypes, myth, or tradition; yet they lived within my unconscious, preparing me for the internal healing and support that I would most certainly need when tragedy struck.

Following my dream, the sense of impending doom was constellated in my unconscious so strongly that I felt haunted with sensations that Michael's life would be a short one. I believe that Michael felt this, too. Once, when I said to him that he had his whole life ahead of him, we stared at each other in wordless, confusing pain. I knew I was lying, but couldn't grasp the meaning of why I was sensing this. On another occasion, I told my husband I had a feeling that Michael wouldn't be with us much longer, then wondered in agony why I would say such a thing.

These strange happenings continued at the hospital when Michael was on life-support. As I sat stunned, his friends told me that Michael had talked to them many times about "knowing" he was going to die soon. He told them he had dreamed of his death and knew it would be in a fight. Later, on the day of his funeral, we found his writings stashed away in the top drawer of his desk. Following is a poem that he wrote two months before his death:

The fist with its all has the power of the wall.
When ended, we will see who will last through it all.
When in need, we will turn and see
What our idols mean.
With the Sids and the Rottens,
With all the punks and nockens.
We will slam and scamp around on the slamming floor.
With a snap and a scratch, we will kill our little scalp.
With the slashing of an arm, with the breaking of bone,
We will go back to the real home.

Jung claims the existence of two separate conscious realities—a superficial consciousness related to daily, external life, and a deeper consciousness that is part of the spiritual Self. There are times when your everyday consciousness has no awareness of what the deeper consciousness knows, such as the impending death of a loved one. The "more serious consciousness [breaks] through from time to time with casual remarks which [makes] it clear that the dying person [is] well aware of the impending end and [is] preparing himself for it."[8]

It seems that my son and I were both experiencing an unconscious awareness of his death that we were unable to acknowledge to each other; although, Michael was able to talk to his friends about it. Elisabeth Kübler-Ross states: "We have found that a great number of children who die a sudden unexpected, often violent death also talk about these matters prior to their death, which would imply an unconscious awareness of the probability of an early death."[9]

As predicted in Michael's poem and in my dream, he was tragically killed two months after his sixteenth birthday from a violent blow to his head. In his attempt to avoid a fight by walking away from it, he was punched from behind so forcefully that he fell face forward onto the concrete walk. With one blow to his head, Michael's brain died.

The days that followed are a blur to me now. I experienced a kind of dissociated agony, through which a painful reality broke: I had lost my dear son I loved and raised for sixteen years; I had lost our future together, the life events we would have shared, and the family and children he might have had.

At our home, the house was devoid of his presence and his room remained eerily empty amidst the clutter and walls hung with images of skiing, surfing, and young women. Physically, Michael was gone, but in every pore of my senses and being, he was not. Weeks after his death, I felt him push me as I tried to peel a picture off his door (he was still angry at me for intruding). I felt him laugh knowingly when I found the sunglasses he gave me for a gift still lying where I had left them five days before at a McDonald's (he was still joking with me). I felt him sitting in my seat with me as I drove the car he loved to drive. I also saw him in my dreams at night. It wasn't always Michael, however. Often, I saw death in its many guises, from the carcass of a cat lying at my door when I opened the drapes, to an out-of-body encounter with heavenly forms of life.

I felt unbearably alone with these mystical and dream experiences after Michael died and suspected that my family and friends thought I was in another world or, even worse, strangely abnormal. I have since found that what I experienced is quite common. Psychologists who work in bereavement settings often see what they term "bereavement hallucinations," in which the bereaved feel that the deceased is present with them, or perhaps actually see a visual materialization of the departed. Psychologists view these experiences as part of the normal grieving process.[10] Are these, however, hallucinations? Jung claims that, because of the apparent space-timelessness of the psyche, "so called telepathic phenomena are undeniable facts."[11]

> The point is that, like all our concepts, time and space are not axiomatic but are statistical truths. This is proved by the fact that the psyche does not fit entirely into these categories. It is capable of tele-

pathic and precognitive perceptions. To that extent it exists in a continuum outside time and space. We may therefore expect postmortal phenomena to occur which must be regarded as authentic.[12]

During the days that immediately followed Michael's death, I was in a state of shock and had no dreams. Then suddenly, when the reality of my loss struck me, a brief image came to me:

I see Michael sitting on the lifted cover of his coffin, his feet on the front edge below, elbows on his knees and chin resting on his hands. He seems fresh, alive, and quite amused. There is an appearance about him that is different, but I am unable to describe it—possibly a glow or different clothes.

I sense, by this dream, that Michael is not only alive, but happy and enchanted with the love and caring apparent at his funeral. It was a beautiful funeral and many community members, as well as his friends, were there. Michael's presence is strong in the dream and he certainly appears luminescent. I've since heard that such a dream image suggests a transformation of our departed loved one's spirit from their earthly condition to their luminous state of being.[13] It's apparent to me now that this first dream came to me while I was in a state of liminality. It's recognizably a dream that I call "transliminal," occurring in the meeting place between life and death.

Four days later, my spirit body is invited into the transliminal place in the following dream:

I find myself sitting in a cave, listening to beings who appear as shadow images, talking about something very important. It seems as if Michael is here too, but I'm not certain. It is as though I have been invited to hear something very important—a plan of sorts—that is communicated as buzzing rather than words. Then it is time for me to leave and I walk back through a dark tunnel to where my body is sleeping. I don't want to return, but I know I must. As I walk out of the tunnel, I sadly turn and see a bright light with shadows of my fellow beings standing in front of it. They are watching me as if escorting me back with their thoughts.

Upon awakening, I am filled with peace and acceptance of Michael's death, but remember nothing of the discussion that I was invited to hear. All I know is that his death is part of a plan and that it is important for me to be aware of this. The tremendous sense of peace I feel from the dream remains with me through the day. Unfortunately, it lasts only one day.

Many who have researched death and the dying process, say it is not unusual for those confronting death to experience entering a dark tunnel and encountering a radiant light.[14] Feelings of indescribable peace and bliss usually follow, or are part of, the experience. To me, this visit felt like an out-of-body experience known to occur during moments of near-death.

A cave is often associated with the underworld; in ancient times, it was the place of burial. In the dream state, my mind or spirit is invited to that place to hear a plan related to my son's death. It is a moment of enlightenment and knowledge for me, yet it is not intended for me to remember what was said. Raymond Moody writes that, in some near-death experiences, there are "brief glimpses of an entire separate realm of existence in which all knowledge . . . seems to co-exist in a sort of timeless state."[15] It's a mystery to me why and to what purpose I was invited to hear this plan. All I know for certain is that I was there and gained renewed hope for a future without my living son.

A week later, I dream:

I am planning for my wedding, but everyone is trying to interfere with it. I go along, even though it is difficult for me. People start coming early, before I am ready for them, and it seems that everyone is expecting something from me. I find myself late and hold people up. Then I walk up the aisle and everyone admires me, although I don't feel so admirable.

A wedding is the beginning of a new life, a transition from one state of being to another. It is a common theme in the dreams of the bereaved. Losing a child is certainly a life transition, the crossing of a threshold you are never prepared to cross. Often, images of a wedding, or intimations of a union, come upon you long before you are prepared for them. In my dream, I am burdened with trying to please people, and I do not feel deserving of the admiration I am given. It is something I'd rather not be experiencing. There are aspects to this dream that involve my outer-life situation as well as my inner, which is a characteristic of all dreams. My parents were going through a crisis of their own at the time, and I felt heavily burdened by their problems. In the dream, I don't want the responsibility of what I believe is expected of me as the eldest child, and would rather hide from it all. The next dream that I have, a week later, portrays how important seclusion is for me at this very painful time.

Michael's funeral is out in the desert somewhere. His body is in a chest and it is in pieces. I am kneeling beside the box, trying to rearrange the parts so they fit in the box better. This is all very agonizing for me. My parents arrive and they are inappropriately dressed for such a deserted, parched, and barren place. Everyone around me needs help, which I cannot deal with, so I keep myself isolated by hiding in my car. I am in such pain and agony, I cannot think straight.

The desert is a wilderness environment where the struggle between life and death prevails. It is a place of survival and suffering, as well as, historically, a place of divine revelation. The burning climate provides an apt analogy for "the consuming of the body for the salvation of the soul." It "is the 'realm of abstraction' located outside the sphere of existence, susceptible only to things transcendent."[16] This desert experience in my dream is related to the deep suffering that occurs when one experiences the Dark Night of the Soul, although, in this case, I am consumed by the blinding light of the sun rather than by the darkness of the water. The desert, often associated with the land of the dead, is where I sort through the body parts of my son, in the image of Osiris. Painful distractions from the outside world intrude upon me as I try desperately to seclude myself in a womb-like VW Beetle. It appears that my unconscious not only supports, but encourages, such isolation.

The body parts of my son in the chest are a stark image of the spirit of Osiris, the archetypal image of the condition of death. In the dream, I am struggling to put the pieces together, possibly to make sense out of a senseless condition of cruelty and want. Von Franz states that she has seen the archetype of the Egyptian god Osiris and his dismembered body very much alive today in the dreams of her patients who have lost children.[17] Its meaning suggests the opposite of a child's development in the mother's womb, which Osiris' chest emulates. In the Egyptian *Book of the Dead*, Osiris is the god of resurrection, and, in ancient Egypt, all the dead were viewed as Osiris.

Three days later, one month after Michael's death, I have another transliminal dream:

I open the drapes to the backyard and see the black and white carcass of a cat lying on the patio by the door. The cat is not mine, but I know it from somewhere. It's very disturbing to see this decomposed cat, but, suddenly, I'm distracted by another cat walking on the garden fence. It is my daughter's lost kitten, Fluffy, who has come back to us. She's wet and frightened. I go to her and clean her up.

The cat carcass lying at my doorstep suggests the reality of death in life that was thrust upon me as suddenly as the opening of the drapes that covered it from my view. Death was on the other side of my covered view, and now I am intimately engaged with it. The image that I see horrifies me and leaves me feeling confused and bewildered. Just as suddenly as death appears, however, my attention is drawn to a young life that I thought I had lost. The cat that has returned to me is wet, as if newly born. This scene brings to mind a statement by Thorwald Dethlefsen: "What from our point of view appears as a death is perceived in the beyond as a birth."[18]

A sacred animal in ancient Egypt, the cat is intimately related to goddess Bastet, the daughter of Osiris. This archetypal cat is the carrier of Bastet's characteristics of spirituality and healing.[19] A searcher and seeker of truth, Bastet is generally represented as a cat-headed woman bearing a sistrum, the same instrument that I believe woke me in my prophetic dream. The cat developed a reputation in Egypt as a moon and underworld animal, and is well-known for its ability to see in the darkness. Likewise, the double lion Routi, symbolic of the resurrection mystery of the Egyptian ritual for the dead, is called "Yesterday and Tomorrow." Von Franz believes that the double cat image is an agent of resurrection, representing the process in which the dead return to life.[20] In my dream, the cat carcass and young cat on the fence are reminders of immortality and resurrection at a time when I feel as though I have lost everything dear to me.

Ten days later, I dream:

I'm in a plane with someone and it is heading straight for the ground. We are arguing over how to get it back up. Finally, it crashes head-on, but we continue to live and wonder if maybe the crash didn't happen after all. We float around in spirit form and continue to live as before. Then, slowly we begin to be seen by others and live as we did before the crash.

Again, I have a dream that points to the continuation of life after death. In this case, however, my encounter is with my own death. In a dramatic way, the dream forces me to experience what it is like to die a physical death as my spirit body floats outside of my physical form. Such dreams encourage you to ask: "Is my unconscious attempting to communicate a reality to me of which I'm not fully convinced?" Some may say that life-after-death dreams are mere wish fulfillment, but this is much too simple an answer for such a profoundly spiritual question. Jung claims that "the question of immortality is so urgent, so immediate, and also so ineradicable that we must make an effort to form some sort of view about it," and that you can do that through hints given to you in your dreams.[21] When the immortality of the soul is offered in them, you take notice and question its reality. The unconscious communicates to you through your dreams, encouraging you to consider possibilities that your conscious reasoning discredits. Consider the synchronistic phenomena, premonitions, and dreams that do indeed come true.[22] If the unconscious rightly guides and directs you in these areas, then why would it not present you with the reality of the soul's continuance in an immortal state after death? When I have this dream, I am in a condition of profound grief, believing that my son is gone from me forever. My dreams, however, show me otherwise. Through them, I am able to see that life continues in many strange ways different from what my overly logical and skeptical mind could ever fully comprehend.

Three days later, I have a second dream of an impending wedding for me. This time, it appears to emphasize the liminal place as the space in which the marriage, or union, may occur:

I am going to get married—it is a small part of something very big that is happening. I am at a place away from home. I had to go there to recuperate after Michael's death. Someone says we can marry in the chapel there. It all sounds exciting, but when it gets down to actually getting married, I can't do it.

The place that I am at is not my physical home, but elsewhere. This suggests a site of liminality and healing. Someone tells me that I can get married there, which I would dearly love to do. But when the time comes, I don't have the psychic strength to follow through with what could help me. Only one month has passed since Michael's death and all I am able to do is cope from day to day. I avoid journaling because it is too painful to do. In pondering the chapel place, what comes to my mind *is* my daily journaling process, a spiritual work that has helped me become whole in many ways.

I am unable to comprehend this supportive tool so early in my bereavement, but not three weeks pass before I finally return to the daily journaling that I have neglected for over two years. As indicated by my dream, it could be the chapel place for me in my individuation process and journey through bereavement.

In my journal, I write: "The intensity of death pervades my psyche, deeply and emotionally, and I struggle to come to terms with something I cannot comprehend. This morning, I felt Michael's dead body lying next to me in bed and sensed an energy on the other side of him with which I am unable to connect." Again I write: "Thinking of Michael all the time. I feel such unbearable pain. Continuous depression. All I do is exist and one day isn't any better than another. Poor Cora, she must feel my distance and unavailability to her."

Months pass and, gradually, my dreams focus more on the subjective nature of my psyche and less on the archetypal images of death. Often, I have dreams in which I search for a Michael who is living somewhere beyond my view. When I finally arrive where he is, however, I find that I have just missed him.

Michael has died, but someone tells us he is still alive somewhere—or maybe he is with us but I don't get a chance to talk to him. Then we hear that he's at a camp with other kids, so I go to get him. When I arrive, they say Michael is around, but don't know exactly where. Then someone says that he died. I knew that finding him here was too good to be true—I am just not strong enough to make contact. I ask if they actually saw him die and someone says "Yes." Then I remember that I, too, actually saw him die.

• • •

I am at a school and Michael comes to see me. Something has happened to him inside—I see a large, empty space within him and then he completely disappears. I am angry at him for not listening to me. My fellow students stay with me, but not much is said about Michael. I feel exhausted and want to be alone with Cora and Ed.

Two months after Michael's death, I gradually shift from the phase of liminality into the phase of "seeking, rescuing, and visiting." Conflicts I had with Michael before his death continue painfully within my dreams. He does what he wants and I am angry at him for not listening to me. I long to see him again and search endlessly for him, until finally he appears in a dream at the young age of ten.

The police have come to talk to me about Michael's killing. As they talk, I see Michael at age ten, lying on his stomach on the floor beside them looking up at me and smiling. I say "Hi, Mike." He looks pleased and walks over to me for a hug and I hold him for a long time. I know that the police can't see him and that I'm not paying attention to them, but it doesn't matter to me. I continue to hold him and forget all about them.

For the first time, I am given the gift of holding my lost child again, although he is at an age when it is comfortable for us to be loving and close. It feels wonderful to have him with me again. Mixed with these intense longings to be with him, however, are dream dramas of every emotional conflict I had with Michael when he was alive. All of the emotions are amplified, as if shouting at me to pay attention to what is unfinished for us. Images of our separation and parting are also a part of these emotional dramas, so that I cannot, in any way, fantasize that all is well between us or that he is still a part of my physical life on Earth. I have the following dream, which portrays clearly the separate journeys we are each encountering:

I'm flying somewhere in a plane and chaos is all around me—I am trying to find out about Michael, I think. I look out the window and see him walking in space with a man I don't recognize. Michael is wearing his ski jacket and appears to be going on his journey with determination and seriousness. I have a baby on my lap and know that it's important for me to keep her alive and safe. The plane is unusual—it's like a flying house.

My psyche is flying in the heavens, a space associated with spacelessness and timelessness—and I'm on a journey both with and without Michael. As the chaos of my emotional life surrounds me, I see my son continuing on a journey of his own. He's quite happy and content, as a man, who could easily be a role model for him, guides his soul toward a new and adventurous life. I realize at this moment that I have a young life in my lap and that I need to nurture and tend to her. She represents the new essence in my life that has come to me as a bereaved mother. In many ways, Michael and I are both on important soul-related journeys.

At the time of this dream, which I have four months after Michael's death, I enter the phase of emotional chaos. In my dreams, dramatic attempts to rescue Michael from his ultimate fate shift to the conflicted contrast of emotions that I harbor about Michael and his death. Following are parts taken from these dreams that span a one-year period.

Michael is in the hospital nearby, waiting to die. I miss him terribly, but get to see him on occasion. I take him to a restaurant and we talk together like we used to on good days. Suddenly, I start to cry very deeply. Michael scoots back in his seat to watch me from a distance and appears surprised by my sudden behavior.

• • •

Someone is blaming me for Michael's death. I feel guilty when I see young people.

• • •

I talk about Michael and what a great athlete he was, but my brother interrupts me and says that Michael had serious problems that I didn't really see.

• • •

My mother doesn't remember Michael's name when we talk and my sister-in-law becomes disturbed when I say how horrible it is to lose a son.

• • •

I talk to a friend about Michael and she helps me to realize that he died as a victim, not as a rebel. I am confused and want to talk to him, but can't. There's a glass between us that keeps us from communicating. He looks sad and despondent.

• • •

Michael is returned to me and has become his mischievous self, which angers me.

Then, as if given a solution, I dream:

Michael dies and many people come from long distances to live with me for a time. They bring a baby girl who needs mothering. I don't notice her until long after the funeral. In the meantime, she is placed in a tub of water. Suddenly, I realize she needs my care and find her floating in the water with her face barely above the surface. I'm amazed at her capacity for survival under such neglectful conditions. I lift her out, dry her off, and begin loving her.

At about the time of this dream, I begin a course of intensive therapy and Jungian analysis that continues for the next fifteen years. It is an engagement in a work of life that Jungians refer to as "a consciously involved process of individuation." The baby-girl image is a new life that came to me as a result of my tragic losses, but, as suggested in several of my earlier dreams, I was not able to acknowledge or even recognize this new life. Instead, she remained in a sort of uterine existence, almost drowning in the watery environment of emotions, until I could recognize and experience her worth to me. Only a commitment to working therapeutically with my inner process finally helps me to recognize this new life of mine, and to love and nurture her into a new-found outer reality.

As for Michael at this time, he occasionally appears in my dreams as the painful reality of the young son I've lost. Mostly, however, he appears as my subjective unfulfilled potential in life and as my lost and wounded inner child. For many years, he appears as a masculine, disabled baby whom I learn to love and nurture, a lost lamb that I struggle to find again and again, and a young boy who attends school to improve himself. It's quite profound how my unconscious uses the image of my deceased son, the greatest image of emotional suffering for me, as the major symbol of my early wounding and neglect, and from there, its healing and development. I realize only now, after analyzing the totality of my dreams, how intimately involved my son's reality in my life has been to my soul's journey toward wholeness.

Eight years into my personal analysis, I slowly enter a major transition in my life as wife and mother. During moments of quiet introspection, I feel deeply the stirring to move to Zurich, Switzerland, and train as a candidate at the C. G. Jung Institute. Then, as if struck by a lightning bolt, when I ask my husband to take an early retirement and go with me, I know immediately that I have to do this alone. I have to release my dependence on and high expectations of my husband of thirty years and my friends and family. My many years of trying to please others and live the life of a dutiful daughter and wife have taken their toll. It is now time for me to do what I feel destined to do in my life, or collapse in defeat of my soul's calling. Some might say I'm going through a "midlife crisis," and possibly it is so. All I know is that I have to go and, if I don't, I will regret it for the rest of my life.

While pondering the strong possibility of taking this sabbatical from my home life and work, the following, highly archetypal dream comes to me:

I'm talking with my friend Joyce about Michael and tell her a dream I had. In it, I go to gradually deepening levels, until I am able to pull up, by a string, a five-pointed star that comes from the center of the ocean. I show this to her and we both are amazed by it.

We seem to be on a journey searching for something lost. On this journey, we realize that Joyce has lost contact with her son, who's caught in a dark, strange land, but she doesn't try to find him. He bought too many sheep, which is difficult for her to acknowledge, so she ignores his far and distant calls. Time passes and I again become concerned about her son. I mention him to her and she adamantly states she doesn't want to talk about it anymore. Later, I mention him again.

She says: "You've brought up the subject of Michael again and enough is enough!"

I'm surprised by this misunderstanding. Just talking about it helps, however, and we begin our return back home.

Two separate, yet related, parts of this dream are significant to the life transition that I am about to make. In the first part, I pull a star up from the ocean depths and my friend, who is preoccupied with and dependent on her family and children, finds this to be an amazing thing. In many ancient traditions, stars have been associated with the soul and immortality. It was, and is still, believed in some cultures that each soul evolves from a star and returns to it again after its earthly existence. A Mithraic saying states: "I am a star which goes with thee and shines out of the depths."[23] A star, as well as your soul, brings light into the darkness and guides you in the fateful direction of your life journeys: "To follow knowledge like a sinking star, Beyond the utmost bounds of human thought."[24] When you are attentive to the stars in your life, you rise beyond your ego and the limitations that time and space have upon it. You go in the direction of your soul's longing for itself. The rising of the star in my dream from the ocean below is a dream within a dream. The star is twice removed from the reality of my consciousness. It comes from the greatest of depths to guide my soul's journey.

The second part of the dream addresses Joyce's lost son, who bought too many sheep. She adamantly refuses to acknowledge him and becomes angry at me when I repeatedly bring up the subject. Joyce is devoted to her family and is threatened by my concern for soul development. An animal of sacrifice, love, and charity, sheep give of themselves abundantly. They are associated with purity, innocence, and meekness, and are unremitting followers, even, it seems, over the edge of a cliff. Often, sheep represent meek, unimaginative, and easily-led people with no backbone or substance.[25]

In my dream, Joyce suggests that very meekness of my nature, the part so flock-bound that it is oblivious to the "far and distant calls" of the developing *animus* potential represented by Joyce's son. My dream ego becomes concerned about this, and it is through that concern that hope lies ahead for me. My eyes have been opened, possibly through my intimate connection with the guiding star, and I now see direction and purpose in my life. The archetypal image of sheep depicts, in fact, a collective, universal dilemma of "housewifery," especially one in which a woman is safely surrounded by her husband and children. In such cases, her animus may lie undeveloped in the darkness of her soul, lost and unknown to her, until, one day, it suddenly cries out. And if she hears it, her life will never be the same.

As big dreams often do, this one remains in my psyche for days afterward, turning in my thoughts again and again, until, one morning, I awake with a subconscious message that spells its meaning to me: "By going down into the well of yourself," it says, "you will find your lost child—your inner lost child with whom Michael is connected. You related to Michael, as you do to yourself, in a detached and distant way. Your inner lost child calls to you. You let yourself down, just as you let Michael down."

Three months pass, and I make my final commitment to live and study in Zurich by mailing my registration and first semester payment to the Jung Institute. That night I dream:

I am pregnant and go to the hospital, which is a combined restaurant/hotel, to have my baby. I appear as a young, independent woman. I check myself in, expecting to purchase baby items rather than having the baby just yet. Suddenly, to my surprise, I am given a healthy baby boy who can already talk and make decisions, although he still needs help from me. I consider naming him Michael and talk to a nurse about it. We both agree that, by giving him Michael's name, people will expect him to be like Michael, my deceased son. So I ask the boy if he would like to be called Keith and he says "Yes." I say "Keith Grubbs—I like that too."

I take baby Keith to my home, which is a hotel. Keith is so strong and independent that he insists on walking up a long flight of stairs to the apartment above "by himself." He's still a bit wobbly, however, and needs me to back him up. Everyone is pleased when I bring him home—he belongs to all of us and we all take care of him.

Keith is an image of a new, independent self, born out of my commitment to follow my soul's calling. He is the archetype of the Divine Child, a recurring motif in the myth and fairytales of all cultures. Such archetypes belong, not only to the individual, but to all of humankind. He comes from the depths into the light of consciousness and is our urge toward self-realization. Characteristics pointing to my baby's divine qualities include: his miraculous, virgin-like birth (suddenly, he is with me), his superhuman size and strength for an infant, and the precariousness of his abilities (he can easily fall and hurt himself if I'm not attentive to him in every way). It is not unusual to dream of such a child when a profound, spiritual change is about to take place. The child is a representation of a *coniunctio*, a coming together of the unconscious and consciousness, and a gift to those who courageously release their hold on outer attachments for the stirrings of the soul.[26]

My Divine Child represents aspects of my life as wife and mother, as well as my new potential as an independent woman. He carries my family name, along with the name of Keith, the son of my friend Joyce, and he determinedly wants to do everything "by himself," my frame of mind at the time. This divine birth within me has the exuberance of a two-year old as he heads up the stairs to the realm of the intellect and knowledge to be gained. My previously lost animus has come into the world, moving toward a new life.

Not one week after my arrival in Zurich, another Joyce-Keith-Michael dream comes to me quite dramatically.

I go with Joyce to das Brachenhaus, a second-hand store in Zurich that specializes in household items. We look for a good bargain, but instead, find overpriced furniture that is made of cheap plastic. Joyce and I talk about the different directions our lives have taken. She's staying at home and I have gone to Switzerland. Later, I return and find Joyce working in the cafeteria at the store. She's too busy waiting on people to talk to me.

I hear that Michael was taken to juvenile hall because he was involved in a fight. I can visit Michael at this store, but must first pass through guards and regulations. It seems that Keith, Joyce's son, is here too. With a lot of redirection and effort, Joyce and I finally find an independent elevator to take to the top floor. We have difficulty getting out of the elevator and I have to pull Joyce out. We find ourselves on the floor that Michael is on. I walk down the hall in the night looking for him. Suddenly, I see, hanging above a door, two sets of silken pink pajamas. I notice the back of Michael's head in one of them, hanging as if he were dead. He's about ten years old. Suddenly, he turns his head and smiles his bright and cheery smile. A stab of love and recognition fills my heart. "That's my son," I think to myself, and walk into his room to visit him.

Das Brachenhaus suggests my many years as a housewife and mother. It's a second-hand home store and my Joyce-ness is so involved here that she cannot relate to my new way of being. She's too busy giving and waiting on people, while we have come face to face with the conflict of my new life. Das Brachenhaus (my life as wife and mother) had promise for me at one time, but it has become old and second-hand, and now has no worth for me. I hear that Michael, my budding masculine essence, is detained at this place because of early trauma in my life, and it is up to my ego self to rescue him from this predicament. To do this, I have to pull my old life as Joyce up with me. Apparently, she must come with me for the transformation to take place. Then I see my dear, sweet son, who is hung up on a doorway in pink, silken pajamas. It's a painful sight to see—this radiant ten-year-old boy who should be actively involved in the doings of the world, hung up in feminine pink sleepwear. I realize at that moment how much I love and want him in my life. I enter the darkness of my psyche to meet and engage with him, my youthful animus, and bring him out of the situation in which he is trapped. I enter into the new life that I am called to rescue.

A year of retreat and studies pass at the Institute and the time arrives to begin research on the first symbol paper required for the program. I decide to write on an analysis of the dreams I had immediately following Michael's death. Not long after starting my research, I experienced the dream I related in chapter 3, in which I encounter Michael engaged in drug use at a friend's house and find us trapped there together in a state of limbo (see page 43). This dream, which I used earlier as an example of the kind of dream typical of the reunion/renewal phase of bereavement, is quite vivid and emotional. I am deeply saddened about the difficulties Michael and I had just before his death. It is a reminder to me of times long gone from my memory. In the dream, I see myself as a demanding and ineffective parent, and Michael as a troubled adolescent who seeks refuge with his friends. Michael has aged in the dream, although he is younger than he would be had he lived. He is at the time in a child's life when parent-child conflicts tend to resolve themselves naturally. I feel as though I have been given this dream so that I can finally resolve the conflicts I had with Michael before his death—something that apparently must be done before I can write my paper.

My dream begins with a telephone call, a universal metaphor that connects us with the spaceless, timeless dimension of the hereafter. I successfully make contact there, but Michael does not want to talk to me, possibly because of my angry attitude. Suddenly, my dream ego is with him, but it unknowingly keeps Michael trapped, sullen, and disconnected. I am completely unconscious of the reason behind our difficulties.

This dream disturbs me terribly. My guiding Self, the sender of dreams, has revealed a shadow issue that I have never fully acknowledged. I decide to dialog with Michael in my journal so I can gain a sense of what is making him angry. Through what is called "active imagination," working consciously with symbols of the unconscious, Michael reveals that he is angry because I have taken refuge in the glory of his death rather than honestly addressing our conflicts. What he says does not surprise me. I believe I've always known this, but could never fully acknowledge it until now, years after his death. Taking this message to heart, I begin my research and write my paper with as much consciousness as I am able to realize.

Another year passes and I prepare to write a second paper, my final diploma thesis. I decide that this important work will be a continuation of my previous research on bereavement dreams. As before, when I begin, my objective son, Michael, synchronistically appears to me in my dreams, and we are still having problems together:

I'm at home developing my dream material and landscaping outside. Michael is with me and we are not getting along. We're back to arguing over his schoolwork and my demands that he make something of himself. I don't have time for him, and he is bored and rebellious. As I attempt to work on my computer, with difficulty, I hear the car start up in the garage and see Michael drive out. It's clear he's angry about having to be with me and is taking the car, which leaves me stranded. I run out to stop him, but he closes the automatic door behind him and it's too late—I am left stranded.

Reality strikes again! I am not able to go forward with my research until I tend to the difficulties between us. Michael is certainly a part of my soul and my relationship with him must come first before anything of substance can proceed.

"How can I resolve a conflict when death has caused an immediate and wrenching separation?" I ask myself. In the spaceless and timeless dimension of reality, however, can there ever be separation? In my unconscious and the world of my dreams, Michael is as vivid and emotional as he ever was when alive. We love and argue, and I agonize over him as much as he rebels against me. I feel confused about Michael and cannot get him to do what I want. In my dreams, he makes that impossible—he leaves me stranded in isolation to face myself and the reality of my situation.

I am definitely stuck in an unfinished situation because I never honestly looked at those angry feelings Michael and I experienced together before his death. Instead, I joined in a symbiotic relationship with him by glorifying his death and making his experience my experience. Verena Kast proposes that we must go through a phase of symbiosis with our deceased loved one before we are able to experience our unique potential in life—the uniqueness that is separate from, but also part of, the relationship. She claims that such idealization sustains us until we are able to realize this potential.[27] This I have done, so it is now time for me to release the true essence of my son. My dreams are certainly making that clear to me.

Three weeks later, I dream:

Ed and I are cleaning a new house we have moved into and I realize that major things need to be done. Michael is with us as if he never left. I want him to help us, but he refuses. He wants to go out with his friends first. We argue about it, until Ed comes in and says to let him go out. Reluctantly, I let him go. While he's gone, I go out into the neighborhood and experience many strong feelings that I find horrifying and painful. Then Michael returns and offers to work with us. I'm glad to finally have his cooperation. He seems to have changed—either that, or I see him in a new way.

By honestly acknowledging my relationship with Michael, my inner Self helps to resolve the psychic conflict I have had with him for so many years. In my dreams, Michael and I again engage in our usual unresolved conflict, but this time, we arrive at a new place. My husband, Ed, is the helper, the masculine within me that acts as intermediary. He provides the psychic strength and security that I need to stand on my own without my son's help. By giving Michael his freedom, he then chooses to work cooperatively with me. By releasing my ego-driven hold on him, our relationship transforms.

Two days later, I dream:

Ed has been tending to two horses of mine that are boarded in town. I realize that we must find a more permanent and comfortable place for them. I go to where the horses are and see our rose garden. I replant a special area and tend to other roses that need special care. Then I walk around the garden and see Michael lying in an open grave—he's been in a coma all of these years. I enter the grave with him and see that he is moving a bit and mumbling. His head is lying in a pool of water, so I carefully lift it up. He talks to me and becomes more alert. I feel such tender love for him, saying how much I've missed him and that I can't believe he's waking up.

"Just keep talking, Mike, so you don't go back to sleep," I say. I notice he's wearing a shirt with blue roses on it.

"I think Dad put that on you the other day," I say to him.

"Yes—he gave that to me for Mother's/Father's Day."

Michael becomes more alert and I lead him up, out of the grave. I sit him down on the grass, take him in my arms, run my fingers through his hair, and lovingly caress his tender face while telling him how wonderful it is to have him back with us again.

In the dream, Ed, as my masculine energy, tends to the polarity of my libido, represented as the two horses. They suggest a conjunction of opposites, life and death or mother protector and terrible mother.[28] Barbara Hannah states: "We can realize our energy, personified as the horse, and it can do a lot for us, but only if we live under the law of our being."[29] The horse represents libido that has passed into the world. I am attending to the task of my libido and cultivating my garden—I am attending to my affairs, rather than expecting my son to do it for me.

Roses, the flower of death and resurrection, symbolize a transcendence of the human spirit. Jung sees the rose as an image of an integration of the personality and a balance between the conscious and the unconscious. When I find Michael lying in the open grave, he is wearing a shirt with blue roses on it that Ed put on him the day before. The blue rose suggests impossibility. It is a reminder to me of the impossibility of Michael acting as my potential in life. Because it was given to him on Mother's/Father's day, it is a statement that he does not have to live for his parents any longer. The blue rose is his gift of freedom. Through the tending of my garden, Michael can be resurrected in the image of himself before he died. I see and recognize him as my son, a child who is a part of me, but also quite separate. He is free now to live his own destiny apart from his mother's wishes, yet receive the love from his mother that is rightfully his.

Close to a year later, when my candidate studies at the Jung Institute end, I am guided through a final ritual with Michael. My dream:

I've been on a difficult journey and now I hear that I have to hand Michael over to his rightful parents. Even though he has been gone, I continue to believe he is my son. I know these people—they are a community of humankind. With much planning and organizing, the exchange takes place in my professional therapy office. I hand Michael over to his new mother, whom I do not recognize. The scene is very sad and emotional, as I stroke him and say my last good-byes.

Through conscious suffering that transforms our relationship to ourselves and others, we do indeed give to the universe of humankind. In my dream, I transfer the memory of all that I have experienced with my son within my professional office, a symbol of the interactive space of suffering and transformation. Michael's new mother is the life principle and the link of generations to come.

Two months pass and, during this time, my mother's horrible illness and battle with rheumatoid arthritis has taken all it can from her frail body. I know that she is on her last days. We talk intimately about death and her feelings about it. My father joins us and I encourage them both to try to make peace together before her death. It is not an easy talk. Neither of my parents is conscious of the spiritual reality of death, let alone the influence each has had on the other during their fifty-five years of marriage. As I drive home, I feel the aura and mystery of death strongly around me and the essence of God deep within my soul. That night, I dream:

I'm walking in San Francisco with my family, parents, brothers. Michael has joined us on this special occasion. He has been busy settling into a productive way of life completely separate from us. As we walk, Michael and I go off alone to talk. He appears slightly different—his hair is curly and light, rather than dark brown. I ask him what he's been doing, how he's been eating and what he's been living on in his "independent living situation." He says he has money and I assume it's from a fund set up by Ed. It's enough for him to be able to learn new things, but I don't know exactly what it is he's learning.

We stop to wait for the others on the top of a hill that overlooks the lovely city of San Francisco and the bay behind it—could be Lombard Street. Michael lays his head on my shoulder.

"I've missed you, you know," I say to him, sensing that he needs to hear this from me. He does, and in this moment, I know deeply that we are both transformed in a positive, loving way through our shared experience of life and death.

chapter five

SAYING OUR GOODBYES—
A YOUNG WIFE'S STORY

. . . forgive me.
If you are not living,
if you, beloved, my love,
if you have died,
all the leaves will fall on my breast,
it will rain upon my soul night and day

. . .

My feet will want to march toward where you sleep,
but I shall go on living . . .

—PABLO NERUDA, "The Dead Woman"

Occasionally, a dream so impressed Kathleen that she would share it with others and wonder about that strange, inner dimension of reality we call the unconscious. For the most part, however, she had only a passing interest in dreams. She was especially intrigued when her twin sister dreamed she was pregnant six months before conception and she herself dreamed of the same sister's pregnancy. Kathleen found such precognitive dreams, and the meaning behind dream symbols in general, fascinating. "But just for fun," she said. "I didn't take them seriously." Then, her young husband, Kevin, died and something quite different and unexpected began to happen in her dreams. He appeared in them so vividly it was as if he were still alive.

Kathleen says: "Those dreams made me feel hopeful about life after death and the possibility that Kevin is still around. I don't have any concrete notions about dreams and why we dream the things we do, but I'm beginning to believe that they have a spiritual side to them. It seems as if we function everyday on the 'surface,' yet there's a powerful underlying sensory system with which we gather enormous amounts of information. Some of this is processed unconsciously, and some of it goes unnoticed by us in our everyday lives. I wonder if it can manifest in our dreams."

Life gave Kathleen a fateful "turn of events" in a relationship that felt spiritually ordained to her. From her first meeting with Kevin while vacationing in Thailand, they experienced a commitment to each other that never wavered, and, in many ways, made them feel as connected as soul mates. Shortly after that vacation, a dream came to Kathleen that she believes clarified her future with Kevin. It was a death dream in which her old boyfriend died. Kathleen knew, at some level, that this particular image of death symbolized the final ending of a relationship with a previous first love that was not meant to be. Death dreams of this kind can, indeed, express the ending of a relationship or the death of an aspect of being. She was closing the door to one relationship and beginning another with Kevin that had meaning and purpose for her.

After six years of visits between two countries, many letters, and long periods of separation, Kathleen and Kevin married as they had promised they would while in Thailand. About three years later, a second, very dramatic, death dream came to Kathleen. Different from the first, this dream frightened her to the core. "It was so intense," she said, "I could actually smell the 'smell of death' in it that lingered in my mind for days afterward."

In the dream, Kathleen is visited by her father because he is dying. Later, she finds his body wrapped in a plastic bag lying in a river that runs into the sea. Feeling frantic, she goes for help, but only her twin sister is there to help her recover the body.

In the middle of a flowing river, Dad's body is caught on a pillar that's holding up a bridge. My sister and I have to move the body around the pillar into the current. I tell her that I'll take his feet so that I don't have to look at his face. I slide his feet out of the bag and can see how damaged he is by the water. It's all quite horrific, vivid, and sensuous. Further down the river, people see what we are doing. I momentarily worry that they will think we murdered him. The

task demands my attention, however, so I have to let the thought go. At the end, we allow him
to drift out to sea, since he loved the water so much.

In reality, Kathleen's father did not die, but two months later, her young husband of only four years was killed tragically in a farming accident. On an
outing to visit Kevin, Kathleen found him alone, his body trapped under the
wheel of his truck. He was already dead, although she did not know it for
certain.

"The moment I saw him, I sensed that he was dead. I didn't want to move
the truck fearing that I would crush him further, so I quickly drove back home
and called the paramedics. Later, when the police gave me his broken watch,
I saw I had found him 40 minutes after it happened."

Guilt for not doing more to save Kevin at the moment she saw him
haunted Kathleen long after the accident. As in the dream of her father's
death, she was the one to find him and, in an instant of frantic appeal, the
one to decide what to do about it. In both the dream and in reality, Kathleen
had to relate directly and assertively with death and then release the one she
loved most into the universal sea of eternity.

Kevin's death was the only time in Kathleen's life when she was forced to
encounter such pain. She considered denying his death in order to cope with
it—to pretend that he was gone for only the day—but feared tampering with
the reality of death.

"I didn't want to go on," she cries. "I lived only because of our daughter. She was nine months old at the time and it was she, my dear Elena, that
got me up and going at the most painful time of all. It was especially hard
to see the outside world continuing on as usual when my world had been
completely and forever torn apart. I felt guilty for staying alive and guilty for
wanting to die."

In profound grief, Kathleen remained inattentive to the dreams that were
calling to her, although she was well aware of the images of death and funerary rites in her sleep at night. One of the dreams from that first month
remains firmly in her consciousness:

I arrive at a large, gray mansion in something like a limousine. As I stand and watch, peo-
ple carry coffins into the house and set them on the ground floor of a large room. I see the
bodies in the coffins, but this does not concern me. I help them carry jars of body parts in

formaldehyde that we set on tables. I look closely at one jar and notice that it is a man's genitals, and this, too, does not concern me. Everything around me is gray, colorless and fairly disjointed.

Kathleen is royally escorted by limousine to the death place and dutifully involves herself in its rite of passage. She observes closely as the bodies are transported and, without hesitation, participates. Kathleen is in the liminal phase of grief now and her psyche is surely connected with the universality of death. The dream comes from that archetypal dimension with its religious forms and mythological images. It does not represent her personal or ego situation, except that she is now consciously involved with death.

As in many dreams of the recently bereaved, the archetypal image of dismembered Osiris, the Egyptian god of resurrection, expresses most vividly the actuality of death. He appears as the body parts in Kathleen's dream, particularly the lone genital member. To the Egyptians and other cultures throughout Europe and the Middle East, the genitals of Osiris are viewed as the generative aspect of God, so much so that it is not unusual for representations of them to be carried in funeral processions and planted on or near graves.

The ancient Egyptians believed that "resurrection takes place from what remains of the body's dead matter, not from the soul alone, but also from transformed matter."[1] Their mummification rituals represented a sacrifice of the body that included a dissection and embalming process. Each part was anointed with special oils and plant extracts, and the entrails placed into four *canopic* jars that were set beside the body upon burial. It was believed that, through this process, the body was transformed from an aspect of the Earth to that of the soul or heavenly matter. Von Franz views this as "a chemical process of deification," in which "the body of the deceased becomes, at the same time, a multitude of gods."[2] To fully portray this divine nature of the physical body parts, von Franz presents a beautiful vision-like dream had by a woman while she was in a diabetic coma:

I saw that I was being carried away in small parts. All of my parts had different colors. Everything was separated from the trunk of my body. Over there lay the liver . . . here the heart . . . and there the lungs. They formed a color game, profound and beautiful. And I saw that I was carried away to the kingdom of light.[3]

In Kathleen's unconscious, her dream ego is dutifully involved in the death rites of her deceased husband, transporting the essence of his being from the earthly to the heavenly dimension. She knows nothing of the myth of Osiris, but it is clear that the archetypal image of death, which he represents, lives deeply within her.

Four months after Kevin's death, Kathleen is in the throes of grief and still somewhat in a liminal place psychologically. Shock and disbelief are the strongest at this time to those who have lost a loved one to sudden death. Emotionally, they are unable to grasp the reality of such a horrible fate. Then, when the funeral is over and family and friends return to their normal life, pain becomes its most intense. The house is empty of the loved one's presence and its life-giving support is gone. An ongoing preoccupation and longing for the departed occupies your being and consumes your every thought. It is during this time that Kathleen dreams:

Kevin has left me and gone to another country. I don't know where he is or where to contact him. He left quite suddenly and there was no opportunity for me to change his mind. I phone my sister to see if she will give me his phone number but she won't give it to me. Nothing else works. I comfort myself with the thought that he will probably contact me in a couple of weeks, if only to see how our daughter is doing. I feel fairly sure that, if only I can talk to him, I will convince him to come back.

The painful silence of death makes it seem as though Kevin has deserted the family with no possible way to contact him—a graphic portrayal of the reality of sudden loss by death. In the dream, Kathleen tries to comfort herself with the thought that he may contact her in a few weeks "if only to see how our daughter is doing." Several weeks after she makes a longing appeal for Kevin to talk to her in spite of the difficulty, he appears to Kathleen in their first dream visitation.

We're together in his truck, driving southward down a major highway. Kevin is in the driver's seat, but neither of us has a steering wheel in front of us. He is so very real and clear. I can reach out and touch him and see him perfectly. We talk together for a long time, mostly about farming. Kevin says he wants to help me farm, but I know he doesn't mean physically. He can only advise and encourage me. Being with him feels as it always did. We're happy and so glad to be together.

About the dream, Kathleen says: "At the beginning, he seems to be injured and comes through weakly, but as it progresses, he becomes stronger. In the back of my mind, I remember there had been an accident. I know he isn't dead, so feel no sadness at all when we're together."

Kevin and Kathleen visit in a liminal place, represented as a driverless vehicle. His image comes through weakly at first, then strengthens as the dream progresses. It may take psychic energy for them to be together, driven by their shared love and desire for each other. This dream is a classic dream visitation (see characteristics in chapter 2), an event for which Kathleen has waited longingly for months. The encounter is of great importance to her. It answers an appeal for help and emotional support, which Kevin's presence and involvement provides. He says he will help her farm, a burden that weighs heavily on Kathleen, but she knows that he is able to do this only psychically. Of major importance is that she is comforted by his words and presence and believes deeply that "he isn't dead at all."

Moved by this dream, Kathleen decides to record it. "It makes me feel hopeful about life after death and the possibility that Kevin is still around. . . .The dream is unlike any dream I have had before!" she exclaims. "When I awoke, I immediately felt an intense feeling of peacefulness that helped get me through the following day without that unbearable pain and deep depression I had been feeling since his death."

Such dreams are a gift to those who grieve. Some believe it is a wish fulfillment or a presence needed by the bereaved in order to slowly acclimate to the loss. Spiritual leaders and great teachers say otherwise, however. The Tibetans believe that both the living and the dead are in a bardo state for a period following a death, and that their spirit bodies can and do commune during the bereaved's state of sleep.[4] It may be that Kevin needed to visit with Kathleen as much as she needed to visit with him. This is made possible by the united energy from both.

Two months pass before Kathleen visits with Kevin again. I have observed that visitation dreams tend to be infrequent, unless the bereaved are highly preoccupied with the deceased in some way. Kathleen's second dream of Kevin is not as much a visitation as it is a portrayal of a process of transition for both of them. In the dream, Kevin appears at a gathering of family and friends near a dam by her house. She sees him at a distance joking affectionately with a large, red-headed woman. Jealously, she watches as the woman says to him: "I'd like to take you home." Kathleen steps over and adamantly states: "If anyone is taking him home, I am!"

"I feel an amazing amount of love between Kevin and me, " she says. "We hug each other tightly and fall into the water together."

Not long after, Kathleen again dreams about this strange red-haired woman, who appears this time to have taken over her psychic state. The dream takes place in "an old settler's yard" where it is dark, cold, and heavily forested. Here the woman terrorizes her and the female partners of two other men.

"She's aggressive and overbearing and wants to kill us," Kathleen says, who considers volunteering to be killed by her with one shot through the heart and another through the head. Fearing the pain of death, however, she decides against it. "Then the redhead insists that one of us shoot the other and, again, I wonder if I should volunteer. As before, I decide against it and watch as the dark-haired woman shoots above the head of the blond, purposely missing her. I go inside and find two men, the women's partners, upstairs sleeping. I try to get them to help their girls, but they refuse and nothing I say jars them from their desire to sleep." Outside again, Kathleen realizes how much this "redhead is inside terrorizing the men."

The seductive, overbearing, and aggressive red-haired woman in Kathleen's two dreams is strongly suggestive of the old Celtic death goddess, Morrigan ". . . whose voice was heard in the wind and who collected souls in her magic mirror."[5] Also known as Morgan le Fay in the Arthurian legend, she is the woman who carried King Arthur's corpse into the hereafter. Her name means "Morgan the Fate," the woman that every man meets upon his death, the one who helps him transcend his fear of death.[6] Morgan may, in fact, represent the necessary limitation of mortal life, which is threatened in Kathleen's second dream of the redhead. She must decide twice whether to live or to die. Both times, she decides to live. Her personal fate is in her hands, but she is unable to influence the fate of the two couples. The men prefer to sleep, as if drugged by Morgan. They are already under her spell, as is her husband.

In Kathleen's first dream, this red-haired woman wants to take Kevin home with her, to lure his soul into the hereafter. Understandably, Kathleen is not ready to let him go. Through their passionate connection, she is able to pull him back to her, into the lake or essence of her being. But the spirit of nature, life, and immortality calls for the death marriage to be consummated. "You may pitch Nature out with a fork, yet she'll always come back again," says the poet, Horace. Jung claims: "Nature [who is not only matter, but also spirit] *must not* win the game, but she *cannot* lose. And whenever the conscious mind clings to hard and fast concepts and gets caught in its own rules and regulations . . . nature pops up with her inescapable demands."[7]

The spirit of death, represented by the redhead, appears in Kathleen's dreams to lure Kevin's soul into the hereafter and to force Kathleen to decide between a physical life without Kevin or a death with him. This is a wrenching decision, but one that all who survive the death of a loved one must make. If not made consciously, then death does indeed come upon the living in a psychological sense, as if they are possessed by Morgan le Fay.

Five months pass following Kathleen's dream encounter with the redhead; it is nine months since Kevin's sudden death. She writes in her personal journal all the incidents and dreams she can remember to help her believe Kevin's soul lives on. Kathleen also sees my ad asking for participants for my manuscript on bereavement dreams and responds with an e-mail message: "I might be able to help you . . . We were very close and these dreams are very special to me."

The next morning, Kathleen dreams:

I need to find a bathroom in order to get changed or something similar. It's gray and gloomy outside and people are coming and going. The place seems familiar in a damp, cold way. I leave it and walk over what seems like a maze of wooden bridges that goes through town. At some point, Kevin joins me here and we decide to eat at a restaurant. He becomes upset because he has been here with an ex-girlfriend a long time ago. I try to comfort him, but he has his head down and turns away unhappily. I tell him I realize we don't belong to each other, but I love him anyway and it doesn't matter what happened. I have a feeling or thought that he is going to die as I say this. Suddenly we are in a room, hugging and lying together in bed. I wish I could get pregnant, because he is going to die, but I know this won't happen. I am accepting the fact that he will die and I want him to know I understand he is leaving and I love him anyway.

As often happens, dreams become more active when you give attention to them. That Kathleen has this dream the day after she contacted me is not a twist of fate, or even synchronistic at that. It comes to her in response to her interest in what lies below the surface. This dream is only the beginning of a series of significant dreams that Kathleen has over the next two months.

In Kathleen's dream, the atmosphere is gray and cold, suggestive of the grief and depression that surrounds her. She makes her way to Kevin and undergoes a transition of sorts, represented by the need to change her clothes.

From here, she enters the liminal space between life and death, the other side of a maze of bridges. Kevin is able to join her here, and they visit again in the warm atmosphere of a restaurant where food is served.

This visitation is noticeably different from their first meeting in the car. Kevin is not here to support her, as he was then, but to express his grief over his alliance with another woman, possibly the redhead of death. He is deeply saddened over their separation and feels he has betrayed Kathleen. He does not want to leave her. Kathleen is more accepting now of Kevin's ultimate fate and knows that, in a physical way, "we don't belong to each other." She has a feeling that Kevin is going to die as she tells him this. She is slowly accepting the fact that he is dead and will not be a part of her life as it was before.

Kevin appears to be suffering in this transitional place between the physical world and the afterlife. Sogyal Rinpoche states: "Victims of murder, suicide, accident, or war can easily be trapped by their suffering, anguish, and fear, or may be imprisoned in the actual experience of death and so be unable to move on through the process of rebirth."[8] He also says that how one feels, does, or acts following the loss of a loved one, impacts their future in the afterlife more than one can imagine. "Don't let us half die with our loved ones . . . let us try to live, after they have gone, with greater fervor. Let us try, at least, to fulfill the dead person's wishes or aspirations in some way. . . ."[9] This, indeed, is what Kathleen gives to Kevin. She supports him in his grief and says, "I accept the fact that he will die and I want him to know I understand he is leaving and will always love him."

Only a week later, Kevin engages again with Kathleen in her dreams and they talk together about death.

We are in a rented room that is fairly dark. Kevin is very clear and looks as he always did, but I know he has died and is back as a spirit. I can see and hear him, while others can only hear him.

"I will always watch out for you," he says.

"Can I communicate with you as you are now?"

"Yes."

"Give me some examples."

"Rain," he says.

I expect that the conversation is going to continue and he will tell me more, but either we get sidetracked, I wake up briefly, or I don't hear him.

"Did you try to contact me before?" I ask.

"I was unavailable for a little while just after I died."

I look out onto the street and a man walks by. I want proof that Kevin has the powers of a spirit and believe that he should know everything that is going on, such as what people are thinking. I want to test him. The man on the street smiles at me, but Kevin doesn't seem to notice. This makes me skeptical.

The man who owns the place comes into the room. He has heard us talking and wants to know if everything is okay. He can hear, but not see, Kevin. I tell him that everything is fine and try to get him to leave so that I can spend more time with Kevin, but he doesn't take the hint. Kevin gets annoyed and I wonder if he will be able to physically intervene if the occasion ever arose. I think that perhaps, if he were really angry, it would give him some sort of energy, but this does not get answered.

There is a very good feeling between Kevin and me, and I have no doubt that he is with me even though he has died. Still, I want proof of his spiritual powers.

Kathleen wakes from her dream and wonders what Kevin meant when he said that "rain" is a form of communication between them. As the week progresses, she thinks often of playing a tape from a tarot reading she had two months earlier.

"I had been thinking about listening to it for some time when, suddenly, the tape deck pops open on the stereo. I find this a bit amazing, because such a thing has never happened before. I wonder if the cat has possibly stepped on the eject button. Then I remember to get the tape out and play it. On the tape, the reader first discusses our astrology, then moves to the tarot cards. I am told to ask a question and pick three cards that would answer it. In all, I ask maybe six questions and one of them is: 'Does Kevin have a message for me?' For this question, I select only one card, and the one I blindly pick is 'love.' The reader's interpretation of it is that Kevin is able to send love to me and feel my love for him. That, in itself, is a gift. I have always been skeptical of psychics, but the chances of picking that one card for that particular question out of the whole deck is quite a coincidence to me. My attention returns to the tape. I hear music playing in the background as I ask my question about Kevin and select the card. There is no talking—only the music. Suddenly, it stops and is followed by a thunder sequence . . . then, the sound of rain."

Upon introspection, Kathleen affirms that she was not thinking of the dream either before or during the playing of the tape. She had discounted the dream as "just one of those funny things you dream."

She exclaims: "My hair stood on end and my heart jumped when I heard the rain. It made me incredibly happy. I thought it was a nice thing in the first place to pick the card, but to dream about it in that semi-obscure way was really quite amazing. Other incidents along this line have happened to me, so often that I am fairly convinced we live on after we die. But it's difficult to communicate these experiences to other people and it minimizes them to do so."

A major dynamic in Kathleen's dream interaction with Kevin is her need to have him prove to her concretely that he has limitless powers now that he is in the spirit plane. Those left behind often assume the dead will have such powers following death. Kathleen says: "These 'incidents' have made me semi-convinced of the immortality of life, but that old skeptic in me just wants more concrete evidence!"

From his research and personal experience, described quite thoroughly in his *Septum Sermones ad Mortuos*, Jung came to the realization that the souls of the dead do not, in fact, become instant possessors of world knowledge or limitless physical power. He states: ". . . the souls of the dead 'know' only what they knew at the moment of death, and nothing beyond that."[10] Jung also saw that, not only do they have the same limited abilities we have on Earth, but they also continue to work toward knowledge and enlightenment after their death as they did in the physical world. He believes there are definite limitations in the afterlife, just as there are on Earth.

At some level, Kathleen believes this too. A short time after her dream, she writes in her journal: "I think Kevin is not suddenly privy to unlimited knowledge or that he can predict how we will react. I believe he is still himself, still learning, and still fallible in some respects. I see that he is trying to help, to send his love, to contact, but it is a learning process for both of us. I'm sure we're going to achieve this possibility as we work together."

Five days after her dream visitation with Kevin, Kathleen dreams:

I see Kevin, but he's in another man's body. He can visit in this way. I ask him if he can stay here in that man's body and he implies that with a little time, he can. There are people picnicking. Kevin and our daughter are separate from everyone. I am with friends, but am bored and want to be with Kevin, so excuse myself and go to him. Even though he looks like someone else, I know it is he, almost as if I can see him from the inside. I feel much love for him and from him.

Our daughter, Elena, plays at our feet while we lie on the rug together, talking and hugging. I know he is going to stay with us. I go to Elena, who momentarily turns into a cat. She is in a tree. There's a big canyon below her. She drops a bit, but there is a wire cone that prevents her from falling. I return to Kevin and realize the canyon is all around us, except for our grassy spot and the approach connecting the spot to where I had been picnicking. I use this to get back to him, even though I realize I'm not walking but floating over the canyon. We lie on the blanket together and continue talking.

This dream is very significant in that it appears to represent an internalization process of Kathleen's unique experience of Kevin. He comes to her in another man's body and says that, "with a little time," he can remain with her. Kevin is not in the outer world where the picnic is happening, but on a sort of island that appears to be suspended over a canyon-like abyss, an image suggestive of the Self, or soul. Kathleen refers specifically to this by saying she can "see him on the inside," rather than on the outside. She says that the island appears roundish from above, while the rug on which they lie together is square. Often called "the squaring of the circle," this image represents the union of opposites and especially the synthesis of heaven and Earth.

Kevin comes to Kathleen in another man's body, an image of her inner contra-sexual nature, or animus. Elena, who appears as a cat, is also a part of this psychic situation. She functions as Kathleen's instinctual nature that sits in a tree, or the personality structure of Kathleen's being. It's important to picture fully this unique scene: a round, grassy island that contains a square rug on which to lie, Kevin as the animus, and Elena as the instincts, all connected by a walkway to the outer world (the place of the picnic). When Kathleen becomes bored or depressed, she can go to this secluded place with Kevin and Elena. She does not physically walk there, but floats through the will of her spirit. This walkway suggests what Jungians call the "ego-Self axis," or the energy field that unites the ego of the outer world and the Self or place of the soul.

It appears that, in this dream, Kathleen observes that her objective experience of Kevin in the physical world has now become a subjective aspect of her inner psyche, or soul nature. She says this is the place where they can "lie on the blanket together and continue our talk." The blanket, which she also refers to as a rug, or carpet, suggests power and authority, or the place of royalty and the soul.

In *Death and the Family*, Lily Pincus states:

The difficult dual task for the bereaved is to acknowledge and strengthen those aspects of the lost person which he has internalized, taken into himself, and yet to accept the loss of the living reality of the deceased. This inevitably slow mourning process can help the bereaved to find a new life, which will be truly free only if it contains the memory of the lost person.[11]

Kathleen has reached a point in her bereavement where Kevin can be an inner companion for her, if she is ready for such a transition. What he represented to her in their relationship may now provide strength and a greater wholeness to her being. Essentially, through the image and memory of Kevin, she can engage with her soul. Her dream represents this future possibility for Kathleen, one in which she actively involves herself. It is a staging ground for possibilities.

Two weeks later, Kathleen dreams:

Kevin and I are on a holiday together. I tell him I want to change jobs and move so that I can spend more time with him. It seems that, once the holiday is over, we'd be spending time apart. I ask him if we can stay longer on holiday and he says we have four weeks, which is longer than I thought. I'm pleased to be with him and we are very happy together.

Kathleen remains with Kevin in the liminal space between life and death. They are on holiday together, a time for togetherness, fertility, refreshment, and respite. She knows that this is an important time for them because, after this, they will be apart. Kevin tells her that they have four weeks together, an amount of time Kathleen appreciates.

Four is a significant number in all visionary and apocalyptic literature. Four Horsemen, four creatures, four angels, four forms of punishment, four rivers of Paradise are only a few of the many quaternary images. Four represents a time of fertility and the gaining of wisdom. It is the number of tangible achievement, divine equilibrium, and wholeness. A popular children's rhyme fully expresses this transformation, which is possible for Kathleen:

One for sorrow,
Two for mirth,
Three for a wedding,
Four for a birth.[12]

In another part of this dream:

I am sledding down a trail through the trees. Elena is with me. At the top of the hill, I get off or put my feet down so Elena isn't in danger. Kevin is waiting at the top, talking to me and watching, but he can't or doesn't want to join us.

Kevin's presence with Kathleen is a constant support for her. He is not actively engaged with her in a physical way, but he is watching her, a presence that affirms this new reality of Kevin within Kathleen's life.

Four days later, she catches Kevin's eye in a dream: " I think he is avoiding looking at me because he is sorry his death has caused me so much pain. I smile at him to let him know I love him anyway. He is so pleased and smiles back at me." Kathleen is able to be emotionally supportive to Kevin as well.

Ten days later, Kathleen receives another kind of support through a dream that takes place at a beach, in the place of liminality. She says:

There's sort of a "floaty" feeling here. I feel alone and different from the group of mothers here because I don't have Kevin, as they do their husbands. After they leave, I am visited by a motherly-looking woman about my age with long, blonde hair, who has a husband and several children. She is in a boat that floats on air rather than water. With friendship and light, this woman acknowledges to me how much her family means to her and how sorry she is that Kevin has died.

Even though Kathleen continues to feel left out of "wifehood" and terribly alone without Kevin, she appreciates the message from this goddess-like woman floating in a boat. She says: "It seems as if she is the only one who wants anything to do with me and who makes an effort to understand." This image of a blonde woman floating in a boat has a heavenly and angelic quality to it, one that can be associated with a goddess who knows deeply and personally the pain of bereaved wives. The Egyptians believed that Isis, the wife of Osiris, the dismembered one, occasionally appears as a boat. In this sense, the boat is considered to be the goddess as the resurrection of the dead. In the funerary rites of ancient Egypt, a boat always accompanied the mummy to the grave and, in the far North, Norsemen sent "their dead into the sea-womb by boat to be reborn."[13] It was believed that the death goddess, Morgan le Fay, Kathleen's previous dream image, carried King Arthur's body to Avalon in a boat.

Kathleen's bereavement process itself may be in a state of resurrection or transformation, one in which her intense sorrow and pain of loss deepens to the soul place. The next day, she dreams:

It seems that Kevin is still alive, but has cancer. I come to believe—like a realization of a fact that had escaped my attention—that I can pray to God and ask him to make Kevin well, and it can happen. I am excited about the fact that perhaps Kevin can get well and am looking forward to praying for him. When I awaken, it takes me a while to realize that Kevin is gone and not still alive with cancer. I am disappointed because I was so sure in the dream that praying can work.

Kevin has cancer and needs the healing power of prayer from those he loves. Cancer is a disorder that eats away at your being, but it is also the fourth sign of the zodiac and is associated with resurrection. Historically, the sign of Cancer is viewed as the soul's crossing from one state of being into another, or into its future incarnation.[14] Many ancient civilizations, including the Egyptians, Hindus, Chinese, and Babylonians, believed that the world would come to an end when the planets aligned with the crab (Cancer) constellation. The Romans also viewed the crab constellation as a symbol of the end of the world, or the ending of life as we know it.[15]

The period of Cancer is a time of destruction and resurrection. From a psychological perspective, it is associated with the progress of the soul. Kevin's cancer in Kathleen's dream may be a time of resurrection for him, when his soul leaves its earthly connections and crosses the threshold into eternity. The Tibetans refer to this period of crossing as the "bardo of becoming," and maintain that it is a time when the soul is very disturbed and needs desperately to focus its attention on the light that emanates from it. It is now, more than ever, that help from the living is needed. Sogyal Rinpoche states:

. . . it is then that spiritual practice has a far greater possibility of influencing their future, and of affecting their chances for liberation, or at least a better rebirth. We should employ every means possible to help them then, as after the physical form of their next existence begins gradually to be determined . . . the chance for real change is very much more limited. Help for the dead, however, is not confined [to a particular period]. . . . *It is never too late to help someone who has died, no matter how long ago it was.*[16]

In tune with Kevin's apparent resurrection, his personal involvement with Kathleen in her dreams decreases noticeably. It seems as if he is not as accessible to her as he has been. Kathleen, on the other hand, enters a new emotional phase, one that is deeply painful and is often associated with the Dark Night of the Soul. Two weeks pass, then she experiences this dark place in the following dream:

I am with a lot of people in something like a huge ditch. It seems as if a volcano has erupted and we are being showered with burning objects from the sky. Panic is around us because we all know we are going to die and it will be painful. I can feel the sharp pieces burning my skin and know this will last a while. Death will not be easy.

Again she dreams:

A man kills Elena. She is a bruised and battered little baby. I pick her up and wonder if I can go on without her. I remember that I had shot Kevin in the stomach and killed him. Now I know I am responsible for his death and can't make the pain go away.

Suffering deep agony, Kathleen's emotional state appears to have become almost as one with death. Clearly, her ego is at the mercy of forces greater than herself as she dodges burning objects that fall from the sky, attempts to nurture her dying child self, and bears the agony of death that has come upon her. She is suffering in the Dark Night of the Soul.

Jung views this state of suffering as a positive one in which the invisible "radiance of God comes to pierce and purify the soul."[17] In bereavement, such piercing is experienced as a volcanic eruption of emotions. Anger, fear, crying, and guilt are especially intense in this phase of emotional chaos. *The Tibetan Book of Living and Dying* tells us that "people who are grieving go through a kind of death themselves."[18] All of their feelings come to the surface, causing extreme anguish and even panic at times. These feelings are definitely magnified in the case of a tragic death. Those who suffer feel powerless to help themselves and may grasp at whatever they can.

Kathleen dreams:

I am with a man, someone I know, and we're traveling through a fantasy-like place that is not especially pleasant. Another man is chasing us—wanting to fight. We rush up some stairs with the man following us. There is a "higher power" above and this power helps. The person I am with can now turn around and fight off the man, because the power above gives us the energy to do so—it gives us leverage. We look to the top and see three beautiful Asian ladies emerge singing. It is very beautiful up there.

Later in the same dream, Kathleen revisits Thailand, the beautiful country where she met Kevin. She says:

It is very vivid, clear, and familiar. I wish I could be back there and start again." While there, inside of a bathroom connected to a shop, I hear several women talking about the man who had chased me to the top of the stairs. "This man didn't believe that the Asian women on the mountain were real, or even that the beautiful mountain was real," they say. "It was too beautiful to be true. He was going to try to see for himself."

Kathleen's fantasy place appears in her dream to be the spaceless, timeless dimension of liminality, the void in which a spiritual and mystical reality is close at hand. While in the throes of the Dark Night, you can enter that place. In fact, this appears to happen many times over in the grief process. Kathleen runs from death, ever upward, and into an encounter with what she calls "a higher power." It is through her encounter with this "higher power" that she gains the leverage she needs to turn and face the shadow of death that has so invaded her life. She is able to do this through her masculine nature, the part of her that is persistent and courageous, and her encounter with that essence that is greater than herself. Finally free of death's chase, Kathleen stands facing her higher power, which is viewed by her as an image of three beautiful Asian women.

About the women, Kathleen says: "I think they are in my dream because I met Kevin in Thailand and it's a very special place for me. Their culture is very old and the people seem so wise. There's a lot of peace in Thailand, which is what I felt in the dream at the top of the mountain. I love the simple life they live in the mountains and outside of the city. In many ways, I wish I could start life again in Thailand, because that's where I met Kevin. I wouldn't waste time with the little things in life, but would enjoy every single moment."

Loss of any kind, and especially loss by death, makes you realize the precious life that you had with your loved ones when they were with you. Once they are gone, you want desperately to relive every moment you had with them, to love them more, and to let them know how much you love them. When death snatches them away, opportunities to resolve conflicts, to live future dreams, to appreciate life with them, appear to be gone forever. Your night dreams, however, give you another way to go back to those times you had together and to appreciate and communicate your love to them. Your dreams also help you see how closely those moments with your loved ones are related to the love of God.

In her dream, Kathleen returns to the peace and beauty of Thailand, a place that is firmly rooted in a spiritual tradition that permeates every aspect of its culture. She is not there only to review her past with Kevin, however. During her stop, she wanders into a back area, suggestive of the unconscious, and overhears the wise women of Thailand speak about the man who chased her. They bring attention to the fact that this man did not believe in the Asian women, those whom Kathleen associates with peace, wisdom, and possibly the essence of life. "It was too beautiful to be true," they say. This doubting man is an aspect of Kathleen's animus nature, the part of her that does not fully believe in the afterlife, the part that wants proof from Kevin that he still exists, and that is not fully sure about the reality of God. It is that dark side of her personality with which she is unfamiliar and distrustful.

Kathleen is encountering a spiritual or existential crisis brought on by the death of her dear husband. Such a crisis compels you to face the profound questions surrounding the immortality of life itself. Stanislav Grof states:

> A deep experiential encounter with birth and death is regularly associated with an existential crisis of extraordinary proportions, during which the individual seriously questions the meaning of existence, as well as his or her basic values and life strategies. This crisis can be resolved only by connecting with deep, intrinsic spiritual dimensions of the psyche and elements of the collective unconscious.[19]

One month later, to bring her even more closely to the reality of her spiritual crisis, Kathleen dreams about it again from another perspective. The dream comes to her the morning after she sees a TV movie about a young woman who tries to help her paralyzed husband survive an accident. In the movie, the woman fights against the wishes of his mother, who wants him taken off life support. Kathleen dreams:

I am in a hospital room that is very sparse. I see a young woman and her partner, who is lying on a bed in a coma-like state. He is paralyzed and has a bandage on his head. The young woman wants to take him home to care for him, but is afraid or overwhelmed by the responsibility. I whisper to her that it is OK, that I will help her. The man knows what is taking place and is extremely pleased to have his wife taking care of him.

Suddenly, I am pulled into his eye so that all I can see is a huge eye half hidden by a bandage. He is smiling and very happy. I end up somehow inside his head, or he has projected himself through his eye and it seems as if we are together and communicating, yet I can still see him lying unconscious on the bed.

I wheel him out of the room against the wishes of his mother and take him home. In the end, I hear an audience clapping. It seems as if the dream is a show, but there is something that makes me believe it is more real than show.

In her previous dream that took place in Thailand, Kathleen witnessed a discussion about a man who "didn't believe." Not believing can be viewed by the dreaming soul as a paralysis of the spirit. In this dream, Kathleen observes a young woman bringing her husband out of a paralyzed or coma-like state. This may be the deep longing of a bereaved wife—to bring her deceased husband back to life. On a soul level, however, it suggests the working through of a psychic conflict—in Kathleen's case, whether or not to aid a paralyzed condition. The conflict comes from a mother who, in the TV drama and again in Kathleen's dream, prefers to let her son die rather than nurture him back to life. Mother is an ambivalent symbol in the psyche. She represents the polar opposites of life-sustaining Mother Nature, as well as the terrible or cruel mother who is indifferent to suffering and death. In Kathleen's dream, she may also be the trickster who provokes her into choosing life and the spirit rather than suffering and death.

Kathleen bravely chooses to rescue and nurture her inner man, to bring him back to life as a fully functioning aspect within her. Suddenly, out of her firm decision for life rather than against it, Kathleen is pulled into his eye, so that the inner dimension of life is openly revealed to her. About this intense moment, Kathleen states:

It is like an immediate rush, so quick that it takes me by surprise. I suddenly see a huge eye among the bandages, speed through a tunnel and into what seems like a different space or dimension. Then the dream goes on from a different perspective. I am not sure whether I have joined him or he has somehow joined me. We are communicating very well, but I can also see him lying unconscious on the bed. After awakening, the intensity of this moment lingers in my consciousness for days afterward.

In alchemical studies, the eye is considered the inner light of heaven and the seat of the soul. Jung states: "To understand . . . one must open wide the eyes of the soul and the spirit and observe and discern accurately by means of the inner light."[20] Through this process, the intentions of the soul are made known to us, and through this all-knowing glance of heaven, "all things take form."[21]

Kathleen takes her man home with her and she knows that "I am doing the right thing." People clap as she leaves with him—her audience? Her spirit guides? This inner drama seems like a movie to Kathleen, but something within her knows that it is very real and very memorable. She has committed to nurture and care for her animus soul and to incorporate him into her every-day life through the act of bringing him home with her.

A week later, she dreams of another tragedy—the death of her dear friend, Sylvia—and again encounters a nonordinary world. In this dream, she visits Sylvia's widowed husband and two small children, and painfully experiences the loneliness they feel without her. Torment overcomes Kathleen when she discovers that she is unable to remember her dear friend when she was alive. Suddenly, she realizes: "Sylvia knows the mystery of what happens after death and it scares me. I picture her leaving her body and going up a tunnel, seeing light, etc., and then have a sudden worry that maybe this all isn't possible and she is simply gone forever."

Kathleen struggles again with her doubt about the immortality of life, but this time it is about a well-known friend who is very much alive. The dream is so emotionally vivid for Kathleen that she fears it is actually a pre-dictive event in the life of her dear friend. "In other dreams about death I am very detached and even when I wake up they are not horrifying. This dream is starkly vivid and in it I truly believe that Sylvia has died."

If the dream were, indeed, premonitory as she believes, there is nothing she can do about it. To warn her friend would gain nothing and to wait expectantly for her death would only lead to further pain and suffering. The dream may actually be giving Kathleen another view on what most religions and cultures believe to be death's outcome—a continuation of the soul after death. Through Sylvia, an intimate friend, Kathleen experiences the death of a woman, wife, and mother. She says adamantly: "How can a family live without her? How can children live without their mother? How can a hus-band live without his wife?" As if one with Sylvia, she then experiences what it is like to be dead and, therefore, know the mystery of life after death. It's as if she were saying: "I, as Sylvia, as wife and mother, am experiencing this." As quickly as the thought comes to Kathleen, however, the doubting part of her again counters with: "But maybe this isn't possible and she is simply gone forever." Repeatedly, she sees in her dreams a continued existence of the spirit after death and, repeatedly, her skeptical self intervenes. There is no scientific evidence, from a purely Western point of view, that can help her with this dilemma. Trust in the soul dimension of her psyche and faith in its process is all she has. It is a situation that all of humankind must face and there are no easy answers to it. Often, as with Kathleen, you are left in the void of indecision until a profound revelation or a world-shattering event confronts you, yet again, with that measure of reality beyond what you know here on Earth.

One week later, Kathleen dreams of her own fateful death.

I'm with my sister and Kevin, and we're being chased by someone trying to kill us. The man has me cornered in a shed and wants to set me on fire. Suddenly, I realize that I am not going to die. The man also knows this, so is powerless and can't hurt me. Images of three headstones come into my mind, one by one. The first is my grandfather's (who has died), with his name and date of death. The next is Kevin's, with his name and date of death. The third is mine, with my name and date of death. I can see that my death is not in the near future. I am relieved by this fact, because I had thought that, with this man about to set me on fire, I was going to die. I awaken and try to remember the date of my death. I know that there is a proper time and it has been decided; but it is not for me to know yet.

With her loved ones, Kathleen is forced into a corner where she must confront her present life situation. Through a profound image "set in stone," she sees that her physical death is not a part of the immediate future—that she will not die at this time along with her loved ones. Kathleen is greatly relieved by this revelation. She affirms to herself that she will live a productive life in spite of the death of her dear husband and companion. A death by fire does await her, however, and it is just as much a threat to her in the here-and-now as a physical death would be. It is the death of her life as it was with Kevin, and possibly the death and transformation of her ego.

Fire is an agent of change; it stands victorious over the forces of darkness. Psychologically, fire is destruction and regeneration. It dispels the darkness of the unconscious, the negative or shadow energy that overpowers the ego with doubt and skepticism. Kathleen is facing a dramatic change in her life, and her psyche is preparing her for it, even though she may not know it consciously.

Dreams, like fairytales, contain powerful images of torture, destruction, and death, actions required for the transformation and rebirthing of the ego. In Kathleen's case, her death-rebirth episode by fire occurs in a cave on the top of a mountain, as represented by a dream she has two months later:

I'm driving up to a mountaintop with people I know but don't remember. The top is narrow, although it is surrounded by fences. We fill the car with purple gas from a fire hydrant that is there specifically for emergencies to get back down. The person filling the tank breaks the valve when trying to shut it off and lets the gas leak out onto the ground. I'm concerned there will be a fire when, suddenly, I see the person lighting a match to the gas. I also see that my vehicle has been pushed into a large crevice inside of a rock. Suddenly, we are shut inside of a cave or building. I'm afraid we will all die here in the flames, but realize the toxic black smoke will make us unconscious first. I feel myself becoming unconscious and roll over onto the ground. As I drift off, I wonder if you feel the pain of dying when you are unconscious, and think about Kevin and what he must have experienced during the last, painfully endless, minute that he waited to die.

Then, I become fully conscious and see a man telephoning for help. He creates an opening in the rock to let some air in and tells the person on the phone that they have eight hours to rescue us.

In the dream, Kathleen travels to the top of a mountain, a place that provides a full view of the surrounding environment. It is also where, in legend, one connects with the heavenly realm. Historically, a mountaintop is a place of revelation and conscious communion with the gods. Mythological heroes often sleep inside mountains and emerge in a renewed state to change the world or venture boldly onward in their journeys.[22]

On the top of Kathleen's mountain, her "vehicle of life" is filled with a purple-colored fuel. This fuel is a color not typical of gas, but rather of wine, nectar of the spirits. It is also highly volatile. At this point, it appears that Kathleen and her companions are being intentionally set up for a cooking process. A fire is lit, fueled by the purple gas, and she is quickly shoved into a cave that is reminiscent of an oven or furnace. It is hot and filled with black smoke that nearly smothers her. Kathleen does, in fact, experience a death vicariously, through what she imagines as the traumatically slow death of her husband. This "slow cooking" process is the dynamic experience of the alchemical process of transformation. Kathleen's car, her vehicle of life, is shoved into a crevice, or womb, of the mountain; she, herself, experiences the transformation through a slow death of her ego. In alchemy, such a cave is known as the "philosopher's furnace or oven." It is the alchemical vessel of the rebirthing process and the "symbol of pure, spiritual gestation."[23] As if in the womb of the mother, the psyche within it slowly evolves into a new-born entity.

A letter written by John Pordage, a 17th-century English theologian and alchemist, describes this profound process of transformation: "[the] sacred furnace . . . is the place, the matrix or womb, and the centre from which the divine Tincture flows forth from its source and origin. . . . it is the love-fire, the life that flows forth from the Divine Venus, or the Love of God."[24] Through this sacred fire of purification within the universal womb, Kathleen's ego dies and is miraculously rescued, or reborn, when an air passage to the outside world is made for her.

Such a dramatic "death by cooking" process often goes unnoticed in the outer world of ego consciousness and generally has little immediate effect on it. Kathleen feels a bit disturbed by the images of death in her dreams, however, and even wonders why she is again experiencing such suffering more than a year after Kevin's death. "Does it ever end?" she asks herself.

A quick look at what has occurred in Kathleen's outer life, however, gives us a clue as to why these powerful forces may be erupting within her at this particular time. Three weeks prior to the dream, she wrote to me about Kevin's death and the horrible pain of losing him at such a tender time in her life. On the day before her dream, she acknowledged the peace and respite that had come to her through her dreams since Kevin's death. By consciously acknowledging what you feel within, you can bring the spark of transformation into the deadness of your psyche, which appears to be what Kathleen has done. James Hollis states: "We honor best those we have lost by making their contribution to our lives conscious, living with that value deliberately, and incorporating that value in the on-going life enterprise . . . Nothing that is internalized is ever lost."[25]

Kathleen continues her journaling and dream work for several weeks longer, until external commitments distract her from her fruitful inner work.

Her dreams again slow to a trickle, but the intensity of her grief decreases and she begins to experience a calmer peace of mind about Kevin's death.

She writes: "I've been feeling a bit calmer about everything over the last couple of days. Last night, I decided to try and relax and think positively and calmly before I went to sleep. I refused to let myself go over details about the accident and any regrets about things I did wrong during my life with Kevin." Kathleen ponders returning to England, her homeland, to begin a new life, a consideration that had been on her mind since Kevin's death. She prays for a dream to help her with the decision and a week later, one comes to her:

I am about to drive Kevin and Elena to town because Kevin wants to go there, but the car isn't working properly. I check under the hood and notice that the battery is missing, or most likely, stolen. The tires have lumps in them, too, and I assume they will be going flat. Kevin stands by patiently, while I try to figure out what is wrong. People are milling about, getting into their cars, or in their garages. I say loudly that someone has stolen our battery, hoping to catch the culprit. An Asian man with a very round face gets into his car. I ask him if he knows anything about it, and because of his reaction, I think it may be he. He gets into his car and drives off. Kevin looks under the hood and points to something that is broken. He knows far more about cars than I do, and I am glad he has come to help.

Then I find myself trapped in a large house, knowing that Kevin and Elena are waiting for me to come back so they can go—I can't recall what I have to do in the house, but I remember I have some purpose there before I can join them.

This dream is important to Kathleen because it comes in response to a question she put forth about a significant life decision. She ponders the meaning behind it:

I can see that the three of us are on a journey together. Kevin is ready to go on to the next point and Elena is waiting patiently for us to continue. I want to go with Kevin but it isn't possible. Other people are going and I'm getting frustrated because I am being forced to stay. The Asian man is one of them. He knows the answer to how I can go, but can't, or won't, tell me. I get the impression that he is the reason I have to stay. My conclusion to this dream is that I want to join Kevin, wherever he is, but it is clearly not possible yet. I have to stay here for a while and help our daughter find her own path. I feel that Kevin is with me. He is unable to intervene, but is nearby and waiting for the proper time when we will be together again. No doubt he knows the reasons and he seems satisfied and calm about the situation as it is.

Feelings of loss again fill Kathleen's heart: "I am not worrying about the moving decision. I feel the answer will become obvious with a bit of time. I am missing Kevin terribly, however. It feels like a deep, deep sadness that I have found to be the legacy of grief. When the grieving is over, sadness is all that remains."

The painful decision about whether to go forward in a life without Kevin or remain at the farm living a life-that-was becomes a churning issue in Kathleen's dreams. The growth-healing cycle that they portray is like a roller-coaster ride of upward surges and downward slides. With each dip downward, a new issue is presented to Kathleen in her dreams and worked with by her, giving her the ego strength and endurance she needs in her journey toward healing and individuation. A new series of nightly dreams becomes dark and painful, forcing her to confront the profound separation that has come between her and her dear husband of only four years. She describes the first of these dreams:

I find myself standing above a large dugout area filled with crocodiles and turtles with no shell. The dugout is by a dam and is fenced off, but this does not stop me from going inside. Someone tries to grab me with a rope as I pass through the fence, but I enter in spite of it. Once inside, I suddenly see my deceased grandfather.

"Are there crocodiles in the dam?" I ask him.

"It's home," he replies with a straight, sober face, suggesting that this is the real home, as if I didn't know.

I wonder about his answer, but don't want to put him on the spot, so I ask:
"Do turtles lose their shells this time of year?"

"Yes."

Then I am inside my grandparents house looking for my grandmother, who is alive in real life. I think Grandmother isn't home, but then I see that she is looking after a young woman / teenager who needs some parenting. This girl and her sister had swum in the dam. Knowing what it is like there, I tell them about the big crocodiles I saw.

"They were lucky not to have been eaten," Grandmother says.

I take this message to heart.

I have seen dreams similar to this among the bereaved who find it impossible to go on with their lives without their loved one, keeping them with the dead far longer than is healthy for them. There is a fine balance in the bereavement process between letting go too soon and holding on too long.

Kathleen's dream appears to be a warning to her, as it is for all bereaved, that seeking the dead rather than pursuing a new life can lead to serious consequences. Many signs in her dream allude to this. She avoids fences and barriers that separate her from what appears to be a place of death, and ventures inside anyway to find that the atmosphere is frightening and life-threatening. A long-deceased relative who lives at this place also intercepts her with an air of seriousness. "It's home," he says, as if to differentiate this place from the world in which she lives. Another warning is then passed on to Kathleen by her elderly, and apparently wise, grandmother. She says that anyone who ventures into the ravine can easily be eaten by the crocodiles and homeless turtles. To be devoured by such creatures is to be overtaken with stagnation. It is a regression in the process of evolution. Kathleen takes what her grandmother says to heart and ponders it at length upon awakening. Is she being shown what can happen if she chooses to remain too long with the dead, or in a life-that-was with the persistent longing for her deceased husband?

A second dream comes to Kathleen not long after, as if to clarify her previous dream from another point of view. This time, it involves Kevin directly. In the dream, she is working in a home and, during her breaks, rushes to another house were Kevin is supposed to be building a fence. Finding that he has gone to fetch materials for the fence, she becomes frantic and fears that he is "already dead." Suddenly, he is with her: "He is standing up against a wall or bench and is wearing a black cowboy hat and black jeans. He also appears to be slimmer and has a tan." Kathleen happily runs over to hug him, but instead of receiving his usual pleasant hug, she gets a surprised and somewhat disconnected response from him. She's also aware that his friends are a bit embarrassed by her behavior.

Kevin is clearly separating from Kathleen. He is not the Kevin she knew when he was alive, but has a new body image and wears the black clothing of the death place. He is also living in a separate house, and is busy creating a boundary or divider of sorts. One may wonder if the divider is a protective boundary between the world of the dead, which he inhabits, and Kathleen, who is among the living. Marie-Louise von Franz writes:

> There seems to be, in my opinion, an enormous kind of threshold
> or barrier between the realm of the dead and the living, and accord-

ing to what my [deceased] father said [in a dream] it seems to be even unhealthy for both parties to be in too close or too long contact. What is this barrier or threshold? Of what does it consist? Why does it exist? The age-old primitive fear of mankind of the ghost of the dead must be connected with it.[26]

Not long after this dream, Kathleen decides to move to England and return to the studies she was pursuing years before meeting Kevin. Instinctively, she knows that this is the right decision for her, as well as for her daughter, Elena—and even her husband. In many ways, her soul has encouraged her to live a life without him. She makes arrangements to sell her house to Kevin's brother and sister-in-law, then dreams that Kevin has left her for his brother's wife while she sleeps outside in her car. Deeply and painfully, Kathleen experiences the separation that has come between her and the life that she and Kevin once shared. Sogyal Rinpoche states:

> You can learn so much, if you let yourself, from the grief and loss of bereavement. Bereavement can force you to look at your life directly, compelling you to find a purpose in it where there may not have been one before. When suddenly you find yourself alone after the death of someone you love, it can feel as if you are being given a new life and are being asked "What will you do with this life? And why do you wish to continue living?"[27]

Kathleen ponders the road ahead of her now that she is able to go beyond the boundaries of the earthly life shared with Kevin: "I'm looking forward in some respects to moving to England. I've decided to study nursing at university for three years, and, hopefully, to learn more about living and dying through my studies. I enjoyed being an assistant nurse for several years just before I met Kevin, but had a much different view of people and their situations back then. It suddenly has occurred to me that this career choice is part of my journey for answers. It feels tremendously good to be doing this."

If you could change what life has given to you, you would in an instant. But you can't. Painfully, you search for answers, but none come. You bargain, plead, and angrily yell that life is not fair, and all you receive is painful silence. Your loved one comes to you, but it can only be in your dreams. You see how healthy he is and talk about old times. You make love together, share your separate realities, and then say your good-byes. It feels so terribly final, but somewhere within, you know it is not all that final. Deep in your soul, you sense the presence of your loved one and your experience together becomes constellated as a living reality in a life renewed.

chapter six

THE HEROIC DIMENSION—
A MOTHER'S STORY

The finest of all symbols of the libido is the human figure, conceived as a demon or hero . . .
changing into a figure who passes from joy to sorrow, from sorrow to joy, and,
like the sun, now stands high at the zenith and now is plunged into darkest night,
only to rise again in new splendour.

—CARL JUNG, *The Origin of the Hero, Collected Works,* vol. 5

To heal essentially and deeply, you must be touched emotionally by the archetypes of the soul. These often-numinous representations present themselves as powerful images in your fantasies and dreams. Jung refers to archetypes as the Imago Dei, or the God-likeness in man. "They are meant to attract, to convince, to fascinate, and to overpower. They are created out of the primal stuff of revelation and reflect the ever-unique experience of divinity."[1] One such divine image came to Sarah while she was attending a spiritual retreat near her home in northern Maine, at a time when she was concerned about her youngest son, Sam, who was participating in an athletic competition in Germany.

Just before waking, I saw a dream-like replica of a wonderful hammered, round, bronze plat-
ter. It was accompanied by the words "it is huge and strong enough to hold anything."' I
immediately knew that the image and message would give me courage to bear the anxiety of

not knowing. It seemed like a gift I had been given to remind me of the inner strength that was there for me always. The round strength of it, the centeredness. It was a shield in appearance, and although that was not its first meaning; it became that for me. It was a place I could go inside that would not let me down.

It did not take long for Sarah to realize that her bronze platter was an image of the Self, or, as she said, "the God in everyone." She had already spent many years connecting with and exploring the meanings behind the archetypal images that came to her in her dreams, fantasies, and artwork. As often occurs with divine images that come from the depths, Sarah's bronze platter was met by a synchronistic event from the outer world. Sam returned from his competition a week later with a bronze medal, similar in appearance to the platter in Sarah's dream.

Sarah's round symbol of permanence and solid strength is, indeed, a manifestation of the Self. Such circles are often drawn in religious rituals and practices and are used in Tantric yoga as an aid to meditation and contemplation. Referred to as mandalas, they often appear spontaneously in dreams like Sarah's to compensate for upheaval and disorientation in the outer world. Jung claims that the mandala "is evidently an *attempt at self-healing* on the part of Nature, which does not spring from conscious reflection but from an instinctive impulse."[2] When spontaneously expressed through dreaming and creativity, a new form of increased ego-strength and balance with the outer world may occur. That Sarah's mandala is bronze is significant to her particular situation. It was during the Bronze Age, an era of great evolution for humankind, that we became a hardened and powerful living force in the world, having to survive frequent wars and a life of continuous death and burial. This metal associated with power and strength in the face of continuous death appears as a gift to Sarah in preparation for what the future held for her in her personal journey.

Sarah reflects on her bronze platter: "Seeing this image is a numinous experience for me, and is one I have returned to again and again throughout all the time since then. It helps me to recognize an inner strength that is available if I remember it is there."

Two and a half years following her dynamic experience of the Self, Sarah was confronted with a tragedy that tested the power of her bronze-like solid strength. After suffering from psychotic episodes for most of his adult life, her oldest son, John, shot himself to death while alone in his apartment. John's death was the third of three tragic deaths that Sarah had suffered in her life. The first was at the age of one, when her seven-year-old brother died of polio; the second, at eighteen, when her brother, Jim, was killed in a fly-ing mission over Guam during World War II—a tragedy that followed her for fifty years. Not until the year before her son's death, was Sarah able to bring closure to her grief over Jim. Feeling moved to resolve the trauma through letters she had found from him, she lovingly photocopied and bound them, and sent the letters to friends and relatives who had known him. This experience was on Sarah's mind during a church meeting and, if she had had the chance to speak, she would have shared how meaningful it was for her.

Synchronistically, the next morning, two months before John's suicide, an apparently prophetic dream came to her.

I am in an upstairs room asleep when a red squirrel climbs onto the bed near my head and scurries around in tight circles, full of energy. It goes away. Later, a larger animal, a red fox, does the same thing in a quieter way. Then I find it is a dog. When I look, I can see how they climbed in from the roof through an open window.

Suddenly, I see my little son, John, hanging from a window on the other side of the room. I can only see his hands, but I know it is he. As I run to help him, he lets go and I see him falling down a foot-square laundry chute, bumping into the wall as he goes. At the same time, my nine-year-old grandson climbs up out of the chute, and I reason that he will be able to climb down to help John. I run downstairs to Mother's and Daddy's room. Daddy is dressed in black and is doing the splits, with one foot on the bed, and one on the floor, as if to stretch and relieve a cramp. I tell him what has happened and hope he knows how to get into the chute from the side to save my child.

Sarah associates red foxes with John and his vibrant red hair, recalling that her husband, Ted, had photographed John near some fox puppies when he was three years old. In her dream, Sarah's image of John and the messenger animals from the beyond (squirrel and dog) enter Sarah's psychic space con-nected to the heavenly realm (she's sleeping in the top floor with a window open to the stars above her). From this space, she sees a horrific image—her dear child releasing his tenuous hold and falling down a dark tunnel into the place of death, where her deceased parents wait expectantly. Sarah expects that her grandson can climb down to help little John out. As her first grand-child, he is a loving presence who seems magical to her. She hopes that the magical forces of nature will help her son, but what she actually faces is his ultimate fall.

This dream could be viewed as a precognitive dream, foretelling the imminent death of Sarah's son. Precognitive dreams are known to be the most common form of psychic experience.[3] Tibetan Buddhists believe that the pur-pose of such dreams is either to forewarn of an unfavorable outcome to your behavior, or to prepare your psyche for a trauma that will eventually come to pass.[4] Realistically, it is impossible to intervene in such cases, even if you know that a trauma indeed may occur.

Sarah already had engaged with death and bereavement when she returned to the early death of her brother two months before John's death. Perhaps she was, in more ways than one, unconsciously preparing for the approaching death of her son, or was being warned that his hold on life was fragile and his death already imminent. It appears that John, too, was laying the groundwork for his death months beforehand. This is the last poem he wrote, titled "Can You Talk?":

> Last night I read that frogs
> Argue around their ponds.
> This morning a raven spoke to me,
> Asked "Can you talk?"
> I replied "Yup," out loud, softly,
> As a delinquent pupil might;
> And thought the rest (it sounds female, old).
> It said "I love you," with meaning, out loud.
> It had a message it said, for me.
> I climbed the hill above it
> And returned to find it gone.

In his journal, John wrote that he believed the old female voice to be that of his beloved grandmother, who had died several years before. As in his poem, a raven flew over the cemetery grounds and landed in a tree during his memo-rial service. A friend who knew John intimately read: "John needed the heroic dimension in his life and, at the end, he found it in his contact with the spir-its and the stars."

For two months following her son's death, Sarah was surrounded by her children, grandchildren, and close friends. She dreamed heavily, but not of John. Instead, her dreams were filled with a deep, numbing, sorrow, and images of her children when they were young.

She writes in her journal: "It has been two months ago that John died and it still seems newly painful. As I begin to accept the actual fact that he killed himself, I am left with his eternal absence from our day-to-day existence. And yet, the first thought on waking is of him, the first sight on coming out of our bedroom is the view through the hall window of the rocks he so carefully fashioned into a whole, a garden that gives pleasure to all who see it."

In her longing to see John again, if only in her dreams, she writes: "John himself said to me that I could be tuned into the Universe as he was if I would let myself. I want to keep this possibility in my awareness and be open to its unfolding, yet losing him is still so fresh it seems impossible to let go of the sorrow. I must remember all the blessings, to learn how dearly he was loved by his friends and how much his talents were appreciated."

Shortly after, Sarah dreams:

I see John. He is sitting in Ted's chair at the table and I am talking with him as I stand in the living room. I become aware that it is an amazing event, but that's all I remember, just the clear image of him sitting there in conversation as he might have done earlier in the summer. I woke after other parts of the dream, now lost, hearing the words, "You can forget your mother and your father, your sister and your brother, but you must *remember me." (Not sure whose voice—John's? God's? the Self?)*

This is Sarah's first dream visitation from John. She sees John vividly as he was before death and hears what seems to be a significant message: "You *must* remember me." It is certainly a focusing message for Sarah that appears to be from a wise source. What her focus must be on, however, is somewhat of a mystery to her. Could it be that John wants his mother to focus on him or the place of his being at this moment in time? Is she being reminded of the supportive presence of God within her? Or that she must not forget the bronze-like strength of the circular-engraved platter that is an aspect of her being, a presence that she can always turn to during the most difficult of times? Only Sarah knows for certain.

It becomes clearer to her in her next two dreams:

I'm going down a long steep stairway in the dark, holding onto a smooth, rounded, strong, steel handrail for support, making it possible to descend very fast.

Bravely, Sarah descends into the darkness of the unconscious through the support of an item similar in tone and appearance to her bronze platter. As noted in the dream, she is able to descend quickly, thanks to its everlasting strength.

Again she dreams:

I'm crossing a bridge located at the place of my childhood. I am surprised to find the pedestrian walk and handrails are on the left instead of the right side, and look to the hills to be sure of my orientation. I start walking and find that, as I proceed, the walk now divides the bridge down the middle. About one-third of the way across, the handrails disappear altogether. It is very wide and cars rush by closely to me. The river becomes turbulent and billowy, stormy and gray like the ocean. It is cold. I am very frightened and turn back, knowing I can't get home across this bridge. I must return to the street going to the hospital where I was born.

Sarah contemplates her dream: "Here in this middle way, I am without guidance or guardrails to protect me from the speeding traffic, and it would be easy to slide off the edge into the dark and billowy waves. In a sense, perhaps, I am guarded from falling off the bridge by the speeding traffic, the busy-ness of the world rushing by me that keeps me in the middle way while my fear keeps me from venturing further toward my childhood home. I am stopped, or I must go back toward my birthplace. Perhaps it is a place for my rebirth into a new life."

Three days later, Sarah attends a discussion group and poetry reading on "The Owl King," by James Dickey. She wonders if she is ready to descend into the dark waters of her unconscious as represented in the poem and her previous dream. "It is a beautiful poem," she observes, "about a blind child who learned to see by going into the darkness so deeply he transcends his blindness and can see. Maybe I need to slide into those dark waves of the Night Sea Journey to see what might be at their center or beyond, but, at the moment, that seems too scary to contemplate."

To allow yourself to be enveloped by the stormy dark waters of unbearable grief and to return from it with new vision is one of the most difficult and courageous journeys that you can ever make. Sarah contemplates entering the darkness of her soul, knowing full well that she has the essence of the bronze platter to help her with this very emotional task. She has been shown this in various ways through her dreams, and it may give her the courage to do what most of us avoid with all of our might. Sarah prays and meditates deeply on the loss of her son, and the universe speaks to her, not only through her dreams, but in readings and poetry written by wise people through the ages. Healing does, indeed, come from both dimensions.

Sarah's dreams begin to sink slowly into the transliminal dream state, a state in which personal contact with the deceased is experienced. Transliminal dreams can be experienced at any time in the grief process, not only while you are in the state of liminality that occurs immediately following a loss. This state of consciousness can be brought on through the expression of your love for, and by focused prayer and meditation on, the deceased.

On the day Sarah finds a Robert Graves poem, "To Bring the Dead to Life" marked in John's book, she dreams:

A TV set is out in the cold kitchen entryway. I hesitate to go out there to watch it, and therefore I miss the program. I have the feeling we could bring it into the warm house to watch it in comfort.

Along with telephones and telegraphs, televisions are often considered a metaphorical link to the world of the beyond. Sarah suspects that this dream has something to do with making contact with John and learns that her instrument of contact, the TV, is out in the cold. This cold place is similar, in many respects, to Sarah's dreams since John's death—dreams that portray a cold or frozen environment (in several of her dreams not presented, she must walk and plow through the snow). On the other hand, she had several dreams in which she walks through places that were special to John when he was alive, now gardens blooming profusely with flowers—a reminder to Sarah that John's presence in her life and her internalized image of him can be a source of resurrection for her. Outside in the world, it is cold. Inside, within the center of her being and with John, it is warm. Through her emotions and in the depths of her Self is where true comfort lies for Sarah.

Several days later, Sarah receives this dream message from another perspective:

John and I are to take math tests. They had been scheduled earlier in the morning, but are changed to ten o'clock. He decides not to go at all, and, when I go, I find the test is canceled.

Then I'm driving on the valley road and I see John sitting in a wooded quarry with his back to the road.

Sarah is unable to be with her son because math, or logic, is not where he can be met. Instead, he shows her another place. As she drives in "the valley," she sees him staring out into a wooded quarry, a place of excavation where one digs for rich sources of stone. It is also a wooded place, indicative of the warm greenhouse within one's depths. John's behavior suggests that this is the place to engage with the departed—in the depths of the unconscious, the archaic dimension of instincts and emotions.

Again, Sarah dreams:

I see a very small old black woman with long tapered fingers walking down the hall. I am above her and ask her to help me get down from my high perch, but she tells me she can't help me. Then she becomes a middle-aged woman doing research on people who have done both good and bad things in their lives. I am interested and want to help, feeling I am one of those people.

The black woman of death comes into Sarah's view and Sarah wants to commune with her, but she cannot do so unless she lowers herself from the place of the intellect (her high perch). She is told that this is something she must do on her own, that the woman of death cannot help her. It's easy to see a possible precognitive aspect to this dream and Sarah's work with me. She had this dream more than a year before seeing the journal ad about my dream research. What is its meaning to her now, however? The middle-aged woman is "doing research on the lives of people who have done both good and bad things." That wasn't my research. Perhaps Sarah must first acknowledge her wrenching guilt, the imperfection of humanity, and the mistakes that being human entails before she can truly connect with the image of her dear son.

A month later, Sarah dreams:

I am at a party where I look at a group of three sketches by John. The middle one is a pen-and-ink drawing with stippled shading of a beetle. Then I look behind me and see John lying on a couch leaning on his elbow, grinning at me.

Sarah is moved by this dream. "John once gave me a framed picture, hanging in my studio for many years now, of a dung beetle that looks as if it's pushing a ball of clay, but probably is dung or detritus of some sort." The dung, or Chepera beetle, is a well-known Egyptian symbol of resurrection. It is said that the god, Chepera, rolls the Sun across the sky as the beetles on Earth roll their balls of dung along the ground.[5] This very dung, the alchemists believed, is the source of gold. In Sarah's dream, John smiles at her as she takes in his sketch. He appears quite pleased that Sarah is contemplating this image and, as a result, relates emotionally with her.

At this point in her dreams, Sarah begins to connect more with the underworld, both through image and with John, who appears to her again the following week. In a dream, Sarah and her family are preparing for an excursion that requires the use of flashlights to see in several dark caves they want to explore. They swim up a river and she sees John nearby, watching.

He stops and leans on a log building in the water. I approach to hug him, but he puts his hand out to stop me, his head falling underwater, as if to say he cannot be touched when he is near.

Sarah is seriously preparing to do deep work and she has the support of her inner family. They purchase flashlights to enter the dark place of the cave, often considered the tomb of the dead. John observes them, but does not want to be touched. This is not an unusual message from the deceased. Patricia Garfield believes that the appropriateness of touching the deceased depends on the feelings of the dreamer. Sometimes, the deceased specifically request not to be touched because they are in a delicate condition of transition.[6] There are many dreams in which the bereaved and the deceased hug intimately and even have sexual contact, so whether or not touching is appropriate appears to depend on the condition of the relationship at the time. In Sarah's dream, she is venturing into the world of the dead. It's a time of transition for her, and to touch John may stop her process. John's active, yet distant, guidance keeps Sarah safely contained and focused on the purpose of her journey.

Two days later, Sarah dreams that she is attending a wedding:

I go to a wedding with several people. I'm embarrassed to be there, as I don't know the couple, and we have crashed the party, even though a woman is acting as guard to prevent this from happening.

This is the first suggestion of a wedding, or union of opposites, in Sarah's bereavement process, but she has not yet related to it. In a short while, the wedding will take on a more prominent role in her dreams, after Sarah becomes stronger emotionally. Perhaps this dream is preparing her for that dramatic next step.

A week later, Sarah dozes, thinking of John, his raven poem, and the sunshine striking the glass bead dangles he made. She senses a familiar presence: "I feel someone come up behind me, put his arm around my shoulder and his red-bearded cheek against my cheek. It is John!"

Only days before she began bereavement therapy, Sarah experienced John's physical contact with her. She will soon be consciously engaging with the feelings of deep sorrow, abandonment, guilt, and anger that are so much a part of the bereavement process. Is John consoling his mother prior to the painful work of active bereavement? If so, he does it in a very loving and tender way, reminding her that he will never be truly gone from her.

That night, Sarah dreams:

I am an attendant in a wedding. We are to wear black. I notice that some wear brown stockings and, since I do not have black ones, I wear brown ones too. I see an image of John playing a bass fiddle.

A wedding is a transition from one state of being to another, and is accompanied by passage rites and threshold events. Sarah is not the one getting married, but she is an attendant, a big step from her previous dream wedding at which she felt she did not belong. Now she "attends to" the state of transition. Black is their dress, suggestive of the dark grief that Sarah is now entering. It is not a white, colorful wedding, but one related to the darkness of the underworld with its black dress and brown stockings of the earth. John joins her in celebration at this place through the playing of an instrument.

Two days later, Sarah receives a significant dream that takes her into a new stage of bereavement:

There are caribou. For some reason it is important to kill two of the females, so I stab them. Then I'm on a train or bus with their red-haired bodies curled up at my feet. I look down and am overjoyed to see them breathing, looking at me with forgiveness through large, soulful eyes. I am struck by the sculptural beauty of their nostrils and awed when they move. But I am also fearful the whole thing will be discovered. I feel greatly relieved when I realize it is a dream.

The archetypal image of the caribou touches Sarah deeply and personally. Years earlier, she had had an intimate connection with Sami reindeer herders through her husband's research of them. Synchronistically, shortly after having her dream, a friend gives Sarah Linda Schierse Leonard's *Creation's Heartbeat* as a gift. Within its covers, she reads that the gaze of the sacrificed deer is a spiritual challenge and that, when you open your heart to that challenge, you become more vulnerable to your wounding. It is through the facing and encounter of the sacrifice that you return braver, more serene, and psychologically and spiritually enriched.[7] Sarah sees that the caribou in her dream have come to her as spirit guides to lead her to her inner truth. To incorporate this image into the outer world of reality and consciousness, Sarah creates a clay sculpture of the caribou curled at her feet, looking up at her with longing eyes. "Like the reindeer," Leonard observes, "we too must learn to endure the coldest and darkest times of difficulty and suffering in our lives, and to store up spiritual food, or faith, so we can survive hard times. Transforming hopelessness into faith requires digging into the depths of the soul, just as the reindeer must dig deep in the snow for lichen."[8]

A month later, Sarah again attends a dream wedding, but this time it is her own:

I am being married, perhaps a remarriage to Ted. I'm wearing my original wedding dress, which I realize needs to be ironed. Then I have on the dress and veil, already beautifully ironed. Earlier, I had been given some old, mismatched, scruffy, tan suede sandals to wear on the way to the wedding through a muddy field. I hold the dress high above the mud. I contemplate whether to have the wedding outdoors on a sunny lawn, recalling in the dream that all my ceremonies have been outdoors. But in the end, it is in an upstairs room. The aisle is not in the center, but on the right, the people all sitting to the left of the aisle as we face the altar.

Sarah wonders if wearing the scruffy sandals represents the down-to-earth, groundedness that must balance the pristine, spiritual nature of this union. She must use these sandals to walk through a muddy field, reminiscent of the dung beetle of which her earlier dream reminded her. Sarah must tend to two tasks in this wedding: preparing her perfectly white wedding dress and wading through mud, the opposites of purity and dark earth matter. Both must be dealt with in her state of transition into a new way of being.

This wedding ceremony is different from the other ceremonies she has had in her life. It is not an outer occasion, but an inner one, held indoors in an "upstairs room," the area closest to the cosmos or transcendent dimension. The aisle that Sarah walks down is on the right, the side of consciousness.

Her visitors sit on the left, the place of the dead. Again, the opposites are represented to her within the wholeness of the rite of passage that is to happen for her.

A week later, Sarah dreams:

I am in a part of my house that I don't use much. I am at the same time sleeping in a hotel room and dreaming about the house. Suddenly, in the inner dream, a huge mass of white plastic sheeting rises menacingly, like a ghost, in the high-ceiling room. I scream or groan loudly for a long time in the hotel room, but no one comes. Later in the dream, I mention it to Ted and he says, "Oh yes, I heard you." The unused house is neat and uncluttered. John embraces me and I hug him and try to comfort him.

Sarah is in a part of her psyche that she "does not use much." This place is twice-removed from her consciousness, because she dreams that she sees the rooms in a dream. From this long-forgotten space, it appears she has released a menacing ghost, possibly the pain of the tragic deaths that were part of her psychic life since childhood. It is an agonizing experience for Sarah as her "ghosts" rise out of the center of her being. These very ghosts may be the psychic haunting of her two lost brothers, or it may be something else. Only Sarah knows for certain.

Sarah "screams and groans loudly, but no one comes." She feels very alone in such a tormenting process, but Ted acknowledges that he heard her and John embraces her. Her process is witnessed and supported by her loved ones. Sarah and John embrace and she tries to comfort him—for the pain that he, too, experienced in his lifetime? How very deeply they share the agony of grief!

A week later, while on retreat, Sarah walks across the fields of snow alone, thinking of her childhood. She finds herself talking to John as she walks, focusing on the beauty of the trees and hills. At one point, she has the feeling that her mother, father, Tony (the brother who died of polio at seven), and Jim are there with John and her. In Sarah's profound grief, she is with all of those she has lost. They are gone in the physical world, but not in Sarah's heart and soul. There, they live on and, when Sarah enters that emotional place, she communes with them.

Sarah's emotional work continues in her dreams, fantasies, and active imagination. During the next month, she loses an intimate friend to death and courageously copes with the sadness of that parting. In one of the many dreams she has at the time, she "pulls the lifeless body of a little girl from the water where it has been lying . . . and passes her body into good hands." A dead and lifeless part of her, possibly dead since childhood, is revived and passed to her nurturing inner Self.

Three weeks later, Sarah dreams:

John is in the service and I am there, too. We're both talking with his superior about his plans. The officer has my apron in his hands. One of John's options has something to do with dog mushing and he chooses this. It will require a payment of $17 per month, and I ask if he can afford it. He assures me that he can. I ask for my apron back as I leave and the officer gives it to me.

Sarah believes that "this is clearly a letting go, releasing John from my apron strings, perhaps to pursue exploration in the higher latitudes by dog team. It seems a positive development that I am releasing him and that he is able to pay his way."

The important grief work with which Sarah is involved is beginning to pay its reward. In the dream, she is able to release John from her apron strings and let him go, a process significant, not only for her, but for her son as well. He now has the option of pursuing his personal journey as a free and independent soul. John decides to do "dog mushing," to drive a sled pulled by dogs, animals associated with the underworld. Dogs are the companions of the dead. It is they who guide souls to the hereafter. After Sarah releases her hold on John, she is able to reclaim parts of herself long unused. She dreams:

I find myself in the large rooms attached to my house, rooms I'm not using. Oriental rugs, fine furniture—a bit dusty and neglected, but still there in all their spaciousness and elegance. I speak of finally moving into these rooms. I take a little girl, my child, for a walk and find her a separate playroom under the house where she can play with other children.

The rooms that Sarah reopens are associated with the Self, a place of elegant spaciousness, with Oriental rugs and fine furniture. Not only does she prepare to move into that space, she also finds an active playroom for the little girl who may very well be the inner child she revived from the bottom of the water in a previous dream. The many parts of Sarah that have long been closed-off and dead are now opening up within her. She is becoming more alive, fruitful, and nurturing to a child-like aspect of herself.

Three weeks later, Sarah, Ted, and their remaining children bury John's ashes under the birch tree on their property and join together in meditation on the first-year anniversary of his passing. That night, her son relates one of his dreams about John: "He looks wonderful, really strong, happy and healthy. He says 'Gotta go,' before I get a chance to hug him." Sarah describes her own dream: "John is back! He is intact and stands quietly just inside a door. I am filled with joy. We hug and then I start phoning to spread the good news." The image of Sarah's brother, Jim, also comes alive within her: "Jim is a Northern explorer. There is a dance and we dance exuberantly and I feel how much I love him." The North is associated with the furthest bounds of the universe, the region of the dead, and the Mountain of God. With her brother Jim and her son John, Sarah is able to be a part of that universe. She walks and dances among them and actively knows the world in which they now live.

Months later, wondering how John is doing, Sarah calls out, "John, where are you?" That night she dreams:

John has come back. He stands outdoors in the snow in a lovely new parka, looking tall, healthy and happy. I run out and hug him, telling him I've been expecting to see him the past few days. In this dream, the suicide didn't happen. He has just been away marrying a close childhood friend of mine who, in reality, had recently died. They are very happy because she is pregnant, and I try to think how we can spread the joyful news.

In response to Sarah's cry, she receives an answer so profound that she has to rejoice in it. John, in Sarah's psyche, has made a transformation. He is dressed in new clothes, has married Sarah's recently deceased childhood friend, and is expecting a new birth. John's transformation suggests that he is now a newly formed, subjective image within Sarah's soul, one created out of her loss of him.

Because Sarah is able to acknowledge her loss, engage deeply with her grief, and take responsibility for her emotional healing, she is able to release her hold on John. Physically and emotionally, he is not with her anymore, but he will always remain within Sarah's soul as an image of their relationship together and as a guide to her emotional and spiritual development. In the dream, Sarah's relationship with John is newly different and healthy: "The suicide didn't happen." This pronouncement suggests that the suicide isn't an issue for Sarah anymore, or is repressed and yet to be resolved. John has married; he has become united with a part of Sarah (her friend) in the world of the dead. A death marriage has taken place, the union of Sarah's consciousness of John with her personal experience of death through her deceased friend. The newly married woman, this presence or energy from Sarah's childhood, is pregnant with new life. This is joyful news and Sarah wonders how she can spread the word, or make it fruitful in the outer world. She has accepted the reality of John's death as a part of her life.

Three weeks pass and Sarah dreams:

I am given a knitted baby blanket in lovely shades of pink, rose, lavender, and blue. Then, a botanist friend, a woman, gives me a quilt that is covered with bubble wrap. Inside each bubble is one of every kind of rose in existence, all identified. I am thrilled and say I'll use the two blankets on our granddaughter's bed when she visits. Then she gives me a whole trunk full of treasures, all miniatures. It will take a long, long time to look at and appreciate each one. It is my whole life in miniature.

Sarah ponders the gift she was given. The image of the rose brings to her awareness its qualities of completion, mystery, eternal life, and resurrection. "The full variety of roses are given to me by someone I consider wise," she concludes. "Each is hermetically sealed in bubble wrap to keep it fresh and beautiful . . . these symbols will not decay, and I plan to give them to my beloved granddaughter."

From a part of her that is wise, Sarah hands the heritage of completion, eternal life, and resurrection to her next generation of children. Because of their dear grandmother's courageous, heartfelt work, they will not have to carry the family burden of death and unresolved grief. The roses in Sarah's quilt are each encased in a plastic bubble to survive eternity. Sarah's roses are a symbol of the Self. Considered the Western equivalent of the Eastern lotus flower, the rose represents a transcendence of the human spirit. It is the living symbol that is created out of the tension of opposites. The rose in Sarah's dream, the transcendent function, is a manifestation of a change of attitude or life within her.

In addition to the rose quilt, Sarah is given a "knitted baby blanket," indicative of a new life that is coming into being, and "a whole trunk full of treasures, all miniatures." She says that "it is my whole life in miniature," a coming together of the images and events of her lifetime, all of which are viewed as treasures. All three gifts—the knitted baby blanket, the rose quilt, and the trunk full of miniature treasures—suggest a transcendence of spirit and a transformation of her essence, some of which she passes on to her grandchildren when they sleep. In the world of sleep and dreams, they too will have these gifts.

Three months later, Sarah dreams:

I hold an infant on my lap facing the street on an open-sided streetcar. I have difficulty keeping him from falling, but manage to do so. Then I see John as an adult. He is wearing a laurel-leaf mask and, when he folds back the leaves, I can see who it is. He smiles warmly.

The Greeks consider laurel to be the plant of divinity and prophecy; sacred to Apollo, it is given to those who distinguish themselves. As an evergreen plant, it also signifies immortality and heavenly bliss. Sarah claims that the leaf mask in her dream is made of *bronze* laurel leaves. It reminds her of her bronze platter, which was a guiding image for her long before John's death. Sarah's loss of John has, indeed, become a living part of her soul—possibly represented by the infant that Sarah holds in her lap, a symbol of new life. Tending to this new life isn't an easy task for Sarah. She has difficulty holding the baby on her lap. Courageous and determined in her journey, however, she knows she will not drop him. Finally, Sarah sees the smiling face of her dear son, John. He wears the mask of immortality and heavenly bliss, an aspect of her soul, and obviously radiates pleasure over Sarah and the new life that she holds devotedly in her lap.

During the first year and a half following John's death, Sarah comes to terms with her loss, releases expectations of John's emotional involvement with her, and develops new strengths and resources to help her in her healing process. Slowly, she enters a new phase in her bereavement, referred to as "internalization and regeneration." It is during this phase that departed loved ones develop as an internal strength for the bereaved and what they represented in the relationship becomes a new potential. At this time, you slowly release old relationship patterns and habitual ways of responding in the world. For Sarah to do this, she has to consciously connect with and express the chaotic emotions that lie hidden just below the surface both before and since John's death. This may seem out of sync with the "stages of bereavement," but there is no set timetable or lines of demarcation for them. Everyone experiences bereavement differently and the stated "phases" always overlap, retreat, and reappear as mourning progresses. Each stage transpires only when the individual psyche is ready for its experience.

Emotions that were previously much too difficult for Sarah to acknowledge begin to cloud her consciousness almost two years following John's death. In her journal, Sarah expresses her anger at the psychiatrist for not helping John more than he did, at her husband and herself for not pursuing John's mental state with greater persistence, and finally at John for the appalling act of killing himself. In a vivid dream, Sarah's psyche is transported into a setting suggestive of the Dark Night of the Soul. In it, she cruises in a waterlogged canoe through dark and icy waters, then passes a towering black rock that looks like a skull to her.

Guilt overcomes Sarah. She journals extensively on a lifetime of struggling with John's mental illness and explores the last years before his death when they were close and loving. Sarah writes: "Even though our time together in those last years had been fulfilling in so many ways, John's psychosis was not resolved. I despaired of it ever being resolved. He prepared us for his death in ways that were not apparent until we had the perspective of hindsight. Perhaps we had even accepted, at some level, what was to happen as the lesser of two bad options. His life was in so many ways so painful."

A quote from James Hollis' *Swamplands of the Soul* speaks to her:

How often we are obliged to face our own bad faith. It is not that we are guilty of being neurotic or self-absorbed, but being neurotic or self-absorbed and knowing it, we have lacked the courage or will to change ourselves. Perhaps, given all this, self-forgiveness is the hardest goal of all. To find release we need to forgive ourselves, to feel sincere contrition and make at least symbolic recompense. We need to meditate on the irony of life, to realize, like St. Paul, that though we would do good we do not, that we are our own worst enemy and that much of what we do is to flee our fuller selves and thereby remain stuck.[9]

During Sarah's period of emotional struggle, John continues to appear to her in her dreams. In all of them, he is happy, healthy, and energetically involved in what appears to be a new life elsewhere. Friends and family also dream of John in the same happy condition and they report it to Sarah. Possibly to aid her through this period of guilt and despair, John's presence and relatedness continue in her dreams, even though she has consciously released her hold on him.

Sarah mourns: "I know that dwelling in guilt for my inadequacy is not the answer, and John's appearance in my dreams would seem to confirm this. How can I learn from the experience?" The next morning she dreams:

John sits down on a sun-porch couch next to me and takes my left hand in his and rubs the sore muscle at the heel of my thumb. It is so good to have him do this and I jump up and feel young and limber. There is a deep pink weigela bush blooming on the sun porch. I hear some-one, possibly John, say: "You must be contrite and willing and then change can occur."

Together, John and Sarah sit on a sun porch where the generative heat and light of the sun soothes her anguished soul. Tenderly, he takes her left hand in his and massages the muscle of her left thumb, an area of pain for her in everyday life. The massage and her physical contact with John help Sarah to feel younger and more vibrant, to a point where she sees an image of hope and resurrection right outside her window. Profound words of wisdom come to her, as if meant for all of humankind and not just those who mourn: In order to change, you must be willing to be contrite, to show sincere remorse and atonement for your misdeeds.

All religions teach that you must take responsibility for your feelings and actions in the world. Through introspection and examination, you become knowledgeable of who and what you are, and what you must trans-form in yourself in order to live a life of true happiness and love in the world. Eventually, such introspection leads to forgiveness of yourself and others, and communion with God. "You must be contrite and willing and then change can occur." Sarah hears these words, knowing that she is gradu-ally beginning to accept her life with John as it was, honoring both its pos-itive and negative aspects.

Two days later, she dreams that she is in her yard with an angry brown buffalo, cows, and pigs. She tries to protect the children from them. Then she's in a cellar with her deceased mother, washing clothes. Water spurts through holes in the wall and a door opens at shoulder level to reveal stairs ascending to an unused area of the house filled with treasures and everything an active family would need. "This part of the house is only visible from inside. It cannot be seen from the outside," she says.

Sarah's instincts and flooding of emotions force her into her psychic basement, where she launders with her mother, an image suggestive of washing the dirty laundry of her mothering role. By harnessing these emotions and dealing directly with herself as mother, Sarah becomes conscious of a new, unused room. It is a heavenly place toward which she ascends, one that contains beautiful treasures and tools for family life events. This special room cannot be seen in the outer world of reality, but only from the psychic basement, or from the depths within. From here, her soul connects with its godly source and all of its rich resources.

A second dream on the same morning reveals to Sarah a similar reality from still another perspective. In the dream, she is out driving with Ted when she loses control of the car, veers to the left, and stops. She gets out to see a sheer drop, then finds herself falling downward toward the city below, seeing clearly its fountains, domes, and pools as she plunges into its bright lights. To her surprise, rather than fall to her death, she lands safely in a shallow rectangular pool, an image of the waters of the unconscious and the inner Self. Sarah stands up and waves to Ted, who indicates that he'll drive down to join her. This image and the one in the dream before it portray the intimate connection between your individual soul and its heavenly origin, referred to by Jung as "the firmament or heaven in man."[10] Through the washing of her dirty laundry and her fall into the depths, Sarah is able to connect with the firmament that lies both above and within her. It is a source that is obtainable to each and every one of us once the decision to strive for wholeness has been made.

Three years have passed since John's death. Sarah writes: "Time has not healed my heart's loss. Rather, I feel more and more aware of what really happened in our lives together. I sense his presence often. It always comforts me and I try to talk to him."

Occasionally, Sarah smells John's odor of stale cigarette smoke, which alerts her that he is nearby. She speaks to him openly and always feels comforted by his presence. Often, however, she worries that he has not released himself from his concern for her. Friends tell Sarah that she should contact a shaman to encourage him to go into the light of death, but she decides to wait. John always appears well and happy in her dreams, so the concern of her friends does not resonate with her. "His spirit wants to be here if it is here, and it isn't up to us to try to send it away," she believes. "I have prayed that he know I treasure his presence, but do not want to hold him if he is ready to move on."

Months pass and Sarah's thoughts of John slowly decrease, as do her dreams of him. She attends a death and dying workshop and the Day of the Dead celebration with friends and family. Shortly after, she dreams:

I go down a path between high hedges as in a labyrinth, and as I go around a corner, I am caught by something; at first I think by a branch, but then it is apparent that it is more active than that and seems to be a man made of branches. I struggle and do succeed in getting away from him.

It occurs to Sarah that her image of John has become a part of the very birch tree that is rooted where his ashes are buried. He is an image of the immortal vegetation spirit similar to the Egyptian god, Osiris. An ancient Egyptian pyramid text reads: "Hail thou god . . . who revolvest, Kheprer [the Chepera beetle] . . . Hail, Green one. . . ."[11] Sarah senses that she and John, the immortal spirit who evokes the scarab god, are caught like Jacob and the angel saying: "I will not let thee go until you bless me." Sarah knows that she is blessed, but what about John, who continues to hold on as the vegetation man in the dream? Does he feel blessed so that he is able to leave his family in peace, knowing that they can live without his devoted presence in their lives? "We're both free to go our separate ways to learn, John," Sarah whispers quietly to him. "May you, too, feel blessed."

One more time, she senses John's odor and talks with him, sending him her love and asking what he needs from her. She hears nothing. Four months later she dreams:

I walk out of our room into a very different house from the actual one. It is so vivid. John's little room is now a big living room filled with beautiful furniture, comfortable couches, and antique chairs in small groupings. It is all very real. Outdoors, there is a young couple with a group of children. I catch a bluebird and hold it gently in my hands, thinking of John as it plumps up its feathers. I have not sensed John's presence for some time, but I still feel my love for him and his for us. I release the beautiful bluebird into the heavens.

chapter seven

A CALLING FROM
THE INNER ROOM—
A BROTHER'S STORY

*Coming to terms with the fact of death as part of the continuity of life is seen as
tremendously liberating, releasing one from the fear of death and opening one
to the experience of immortality.*

—STANISLAV GROF, *The Stormy Search for the Self*

Your loved ones do indeed live within your soul after death, and before as well. They are a life force in you, grounded on the relationship you had with them and who they represented to you while they were alive. Upon death, their essence may become stronger and even more persistent in the nightly world of your dreams. They may come to you as the daimons who carry your destinies, or as soul guides who lead you toward the uniqueness and wholeness of your true calling, which, if ignored, may wreak havoc in your life.

Peter's dream story is one such account. His younger brother, Mark, was revealed as a vital part of his soul upon his death, an energy lost and buried since early childhood. Their lives began on a ten-acre ranch in the Rocky Mountains of Colorado. Because of their geographic isolation, the two boys shared a childhood separate from the greater community of children their age.

Peter and Mark's play was enmeshed during these formative years, and often, they took the unhappiness they felt out on each other through war battles and gun play. Their father's alcoholism and macho attitude only amplified the tension between them.

Each boy tried in his own way to be the "man that Daddy wanted," which slowly whittled away the natural sensitivity of their natures in very different ways. Peter was frightened of his overbearing and punitive father, more so for Mark than for himself. When Mark was disciplined, Peter cried and, because of his tears, he too would be whipped "for being such a baby." Their older brother, Robert, was a great deal like their father, accentuating the masculine stoicism and insensitivity that became the spoken and unspoken tone in the family.

Mark managed to remain distant from his father's overbearing discipline. He was more mild-mannered and less competitive than his two older brothers, and somewhat of an artist and caretaker by nature. During his adolescent and young adult years, Mark tended to his parents' needs by driving his alcoholic father on errands and watching out for his codependent mother. He served with high honors in the army, then made Indian jewelry and experimented with LSD, much to the chagrin of his parents and older brothers.

Mark became quite spiritual at this time, an experience common to those who experiment with psychedelics. Peter says: "It was as if he had found God through these drugs. He became spiritual and was interested in at least one Indian guru—Baba somebody—and tried to get me interested in this spiritual stuff. I didn't take him seriously and thought it was only the drugs talking. He also talked a lot about love—how God loved me—and I didn't take that too seriously either."

Mark's spiritual nature bothered Peter. He judged it to be nonsense—a failure of manhood. He preferred the rough and tumble life of aggression and professional achievement. "I was very quick-tempered and judgmental, like my father, and used to get into arguments with him all the time." Peter traveled extensively as a photo-journalist, and eventually settled in Thailand, the country he loved most and the one furthest from his alcoholic family.

Peter learned early in childhood that success as a professional was the road to happiness. Work and a long-term relationship kept Peter busy in Thailand; but his happiness was shattered when he discovered that the woman he thought he loved and on whom he depended really didn't love him. This left him in a state of confusion. To cope, he broke from the work routine and ventured into seclusion for several weeks. Near the end of his time alone, an aura of new beginnings permeated the air around him, Songkran (Thai New Year) was being celebrated in the streets. The stirring of new beginnings in his psyche and the world around him, coupled with the introverted atmosphere of his retreat, took Peter into intimate contact with the quietness of his soul.

Peter had an avid interest in his dreams and had begun recording them religiously in early adulthood. This may have been the only spiritually significant connection he shared with Mark. While on retreat, a profoundly impressive and somewhat fateful dream came to Peter. He titled it: "Mark Has a Large, Secret Inner Life."

A huge storm has somehow opened up a large, secret room that Mark had dug under the ground. It is a nice, large well-furnished room. Mark seems to be dead, but his room has revealed a large, secret (inner?) life—a life I never knew he had or ever lived.

Peter's dream may be considered a "big" dream. Big dreams address major archetypal stirrings about the unlived potential in your outer life. A huge storm, Peter's present crisis, has opened, or revealed a secret room to him that contains precious and valuable furniture. Peter says that the room appears to be a large, white, monk's room, simply furnished with mahogany—"furniture built to last." "It's a perfect place to meditate and to dream," he says. It also contains precious paintings by Hieronymus Bosch and Salvador Dali.

Sparked by his crisis, a secret part of Peter's inner Self is revealed in this dream as a soul place, long hidden and closed off—stored away for a time when he could acknowledge and own it. The place is connected in some mysterious way to Mark, the dreamer and artist interested in spiritual matters. The dream is also somewhat prophetic, because, thirteen years later, Mark is suddenly stricken with lymphatic cancer and dies shortly after his diagnosis. Peter's dream may have prophesied that, upon Mark's death, this room, the soul place in Peter's psyche most like Mark, would open to him. Through his love and acceptance of Mark, he would find his inner truth.

The period between Mark's diagnosis and death was a painfully difficult time for Peter, who was living in Thailand with his new wife. He received few details about Mark's illness and had difficulty maintaining contact with his family. As before, Peter had been recording his dreams quite regularly, and he used them now for the support he needed. Occasionally, his dreams spoke to him as if from a wise source. While in a state of deep sadness and confusion over his brother's condition, he received a "spoken" dream message, in a drama-like sequence about death's calling.

Mark is dying. Basically he is a good boy/guy. The "black road" has been incorporated into President Bush's speech and is declaimed as death road or death highway in some of his speeches—as in "we want to protect you from death road or highway." Of course, no one believes him as everyone knows that it is impossible to save oneself from death's road. We all have to travel it eventually.

"When will he die?" I ask.

"Within this year."

In response to emotional suffering, the unconscious does provide comfort, even though it may not be what we'd like to hear. President Bush, Peter's ruling ego function, proclaims death as a threat to be fought. How typical that the Westernized ego's perception of death is viewed as a threat to be overcome! Another source within Peter's psyche, the "we" of the collective, knows otherwise, however. It says that death is only the next step in the course of life, suggesting it is now Mark's next step and that, when the time comes, we all must travel that path. That Mark will indeed die soon comes across as a matter-of-fact proclamation from what appears to be a wise and collective source.

As Mark's condition worsens, Peter flies to the States to be at his bedside. He spends the final day with Mark, silently telling him that he loves him and that it is okay to let go. Mark dies peacefully shortly after his visit. Grief strikes Peter deeply. The drive back to his hotel is agonizingly difficult—one of the hardest things he's ever had to do. Of the moment, Peter later says: "I felt in total shock and confusion. It was as if a heavy blanket had been placed over my shoulders and head, weighing me down. It took several months for that blanket finally to be lifted, just a little at a time."

Three days following Mark's death, Peter dreams what he later titles, "The Bottom of a Mineshaft."

I have to pay soldiers/officers at the bottom of a mineshaft. We have a hard time getting down there because there are many people coming from the other direction. We finally make it. At first,

I think we are going to have to work down there, smashing rocks, etc., but then I find out that it is a payroll line. I also have candy to give these officers. I have a difficult time making the right change (for the payroll I receive?). I have a big roll of bills in my pocket.

The dark tunnel, death passage, or passageway that connects the physical with the underworld appears to Peter in his first dream following Mark's death. The passageway he experiences delves deeply into the earth, as if it were a grave. He does not enter this place alone, but has a female companion with him, who he says, could be his wife. Peter has the supportive feminine qualities with him.

About the people coming out of the shaft, Peter says: "They seem to be people who are terrified of something they are trying to escape. It could be claustrophobia or a fear of getting trapped down there." Indeed, entering the tunnel of death, a psychological state of being, is a terrifying experience and emotional forces work against it.

Once Peter arrives at the bottom of this grave-like place, he finds that it requires a payment of sorts, rather than the physical labor of breaking down rocks that he expected he'd have to do. "I have to pay in more ways than one," Peter states, "but I have a problem with it, because I don't have the right change. My bills are too large and have to be broken down." Peter has been recording and working with his dreams on occasion, which could represent the bankroll of bills that he has with him. However, the work he has been doing is not done thoroughly enough to get him through the tunnel. Peter has much work to do before he can "see the light at the end of the tunnel."

Peter has deep, psychological work to do. He must break down his elemental nature and chip away at his resources, his dreams, before he can come to the place of his deceased brother, with whom secrets of the inner room are concealed.

Three days later, Peter dreams about what he calls, his "attitude problem."

I am chosen by one of the princesses to be one of her escorts to help her lose her virginity. But just when we are about to leave the group of 250, her mother (my wife's aunt) calls me out and informs me that, because of my attitude, I should not go with her. She says that I should also leave my job because of my attitude. I tell her that I have been working very hard, but I agree that, if within a couple of months, my attitude hasn't changed, I will quit.

"But what will you do?" she asks almost triumphantly and in a challenging manner. I say that I will probably return to the States. Her triumphant smile fades. I feel very heavy-hearted when I leave the group and begin walking home to tell my wife the news. I realize that I must stop working so hard and stop taking pills in order to work and to change my attitude if I am to stay in Thailand.

Religious worship in the ancient civilizations of Greece, Rome, and India involved what is called "sacred prostitution." In Greece, these prostitutes were known as *hierodules* and were considered an embodiment of the Great Goddess. After passing puberty, young girls were offered to the temple for sexual intercourse. They were trained by priestesses and, before they could leave, had to unite sexually with at least one man. This sexual intercourse represented a union between the male and female aspects of being, that which completes the process of purification or wholeness. It was believed that sacred whores mellowed the nature of humankind and nurtured the eternal source of creativity.

In the myth, Gilgamesh's wild-man counterpart, Enkidu, became civilized, wise, and understanding after having sexual intercourse with a hierodule sent by Gilgamesh. At that point, Gilgamesh's nature became more whole and unified. Caitlin Matthews states:

> The experience of the bridal chamber, the "little death" of orgasm where union is experienced as a temporary death of the ego, was a profound mystery of non-duality and therefore of spiritual illumination. The initiate's journey was as mysterious as the passage of the virgin beyond the gates of the hymen.[1]

Peter's psychological involvement in a virginity ritual suggests an offering of this union to him. The time is erotic and ripe for Peter while in this liminal state of being six days following his brother's death, but his psyche is not ready for such a momentous union. In the dream, the young woman's mother, represented as his wife's aunt, says that he has an "attitude problem."

Peter's aunt by marriage "is a greedy person, one who is always looking for ways to make a buck," he says. "She is always selling something expensive, and my wife is always buying. She is also a figure of authority, a doctor, and a woman with whom I worked." The dominant authority, healing, and ever-greedy feminine nature of Peter expects and demands more from him than what he has done so far in his life. It challenges him to change his attitude, which has become "angry and bitter." "I need to soften my attitude, soften my heart," he says.

In the dream, Peter courageously interacts with this challenge by saying he will quit his job if his attitude does not change. The triumphant feminine-as-trickster encourages him to become even more conscious by asking: "What will you do then?" "Probably go back to the States," he responds. Feeling defeated by this thought, Peter retreats from the sacred ritual and its promise of potential wholeness with a heavy heart.

Thoughts of a lifestyle change flood Peter's consciousness. He considers dealing more consciously with the pill dependence that keeps him going and changing his angry and bitter attitude. Peter knows instinctively that these changes require his leaving the unfulfilling and outwardly demanding job he has had for years. He knows this is necessary if he wants to engage in the psychological state of what Thailand represents to him. Peter claims: "Returning to the States is like returning to the bad, old past. It's a kind of regression (the alternate option from growth). Being in Thailand is like being in the ever-changing present, where something new and different is going on all the time."

Three weeks later, shortly after returning to his home in Thailand following Mark's funeral, Mark appears to Peter for the first time in a dream. It is a reminder to Peter of his bad attitude and the sacred prostitute that has become a part of his new psychic situation.

My older brother buys Mark a present and I want him to buy me one too. Specifically, I am interested in a .22 caliber rifle. We walk around and around the store looking at these guns. Mark tells me that he is going to tell his prostitute girlfriends that I am his brother. I don't want him to do this.

Peter's dream ego continues to prefer anger and aggression, as represented by his desire for a .22 caliber rifle, a weapon he played with in childhood and occasionally used to control Mark. The number 22 is often represented as a type of gun in dreams. Why specifically 22? Universally, the number represents a superfluity or overabundance of the lucky number 21. Its essence is folly and arrogance, and this is what he wants his big brother to give him. Peter walks "around and around" this child-like, arrogant, angry attitude until Mark brings up the subject of his "prostitute girlfriends." He reminds Peter about them, indicating his connection to and involvement with these "sacred whores." Is he suggesting to Peter that they are waiting for him? Peter doesn't want to think about it. He isn't ready for such a sacred union. Are we ever ready when the soul calls to us?

Five days later, Peter dreams what he titles: "Mark is Dead:"

I want to do this trick where Mark and Robert and I jump/fall into a swimming pool together. When Mark and I do it with someone else (his first wife), Mark appears to be seriously injured. I want to do this with my two brothers because I think it would be neat, but Robert and his wife don't want me/us to do it. Then I realize that we can't do it because Mark is dead. Mark is injured, not in the fall into the pool, but afterward getting out. He becomes disoriented and falls onto the concrete.

Peter is ready to take a leap into the pool or water of life, his emotions, but seems to have problems coordinating this with the brothers he feels he needs. He wants his older brother to join him and Mark, and for the three of them to fall together as a unit. This is not Robert's character, however. According to Peter, Robert "doesn't like to face unpleasant things." His life is primarily focused on the material level and the latest computer technology.

"I don't think Robert really wants to talk about Mark's death at all. I need to talk about his death with him—with somebody—but he doesn't really want to face his depression, his sadness, or my depression, my sadness, so we don't." Robert is driven by worldly things and avoids the emotional aspect of life. It's clear that Peter has to take the plunge without him.

An important element to consider in this fall is the "someone else" who joins them—the someone else who causes Mark to be injured. According to Peter, she appears to be Mark's ex-wife, a woman who did not accept his spiritual and creative essence when he was alive. Peter believes that Mark's divorce left him badly hurt psychologically, that he lost his confidence (fell) and became depressed. "I think the concrete here refers to the hard reality that Mark faced." Indeed, such a fall can cause disorientation and a knock with the hard reality of life. Because this is Peter's dream, however, the fall referred to here is most likely Peter's fall into depression as a result of Mark's death.

The realization of how alone Peter truly feels becomes even more evident to him when he remembers that "Mark is dead." He has no ego-driven older brother or spiritually aware younger brother to accompany him on his journey inward. "Mark is Dead," he remembers. Is his death a hindrance to Peter? Jung writes:

> . . . a deadly longing for the abyss, a longing to drown in his own source, to be sucked down to the realm of the Mothers. . . . This death is no external enemy, it is his own inner longing for the stillness and profound peace of all-knowing non-existence, for all-seeing sleep in the ocean of coming-to-be and passing away.[2]

Not four weeks pass before Peter is reminded quite strongly again in a dream that he should take the previous "Mark is Dead" dream seriously. He titles his dream, "Inconsolable."

I have a dream that Robert is sick in one of my dreams. Then he dies and I am heartbroken that I did not listen to my previous dream. I am inconsolable. The dream this refers to is the one where we are all in the swimming pool and I want them to jump off my shoulders into the water.

Robert is that aspect of Peter that does not want to jump into the water of life—the part that avoids emotional and spiritual matters. From the viewpoint of the Self, this feature of Peter has been sick and it is now dead, or gone. Peter is heartbroken over it, believing that, if he had noticed Robert was sick in the dream, he might have been able to do something about it. The ego-driven Robert side of Peter has died. Deep grief overcomes him when he realizes that he has again suffered a tragic loss. This time, however, it is a loss of ego. The pool of water represents introversion, a descent into the darkness of the unconscious. You must first go underground before the *hieros gamos*, or sacred union, can occur.

Six weeks after Mark's death, Peter returns to his work in Thailand. Feelings of illness and depression make him realize that he should have taken a longer leave. "It's as if I'm still partly under a cloud or blanket that pretty much surrounds me all of the time. How long will it be before I stop being so oppressed by my sadness?"

Discomfort over his life's focus begins to haunt Peter, until he realizes deep within that he can't continue working in his job any longer. "But how can I quit? What would I do? A man 'has to' have a job to earn money!" Drinking becomes more a part of Peter's life as he drifts in and out of depression. In his dreams, the essence of death dwells strongly within.

"We are visiting the police station where it is suspected that Mark was tortured before he died."

• • •

"I find myself high up in the mountains on a narrow trail. A dog goes bounding by me. I hear his footsteps and am momentarily afraid."

• • •

"Trying to bury Mark. They won't let him be buried because they think he killed himself. I say, 'No, he died of AIDS.'"

To ease his suffering, Peter takes a leave from his job and house-sits for his brother back in the States. After a month of introversion and quiet seclusion in this place away from home, he finally decides to quit the job that has preyed on him for so many years. In his journal, he writes: "I thought that it was the job that was killing me, but it could have been my inability to face my sadness, my grief over Mark's death."

Writing and dream work become Peter's preoccupation, and his dreams respond with intensity. In one, he is in an earthquake that dislodges an apartment building on the side of a hill with Mark in it. The building slides down after him as he and Mark run in front of it. Then, Mark laughs when Peter sees a car partly crushed by the sliding building. Peter's mobility (car) has become demolished by the shake-up in his outer life and it appears that Mark finds this amusing.

In another dream, Peter has "a pony tail of hair of which I am very proud. I wrestle with Mark on the front lawn." Reminiscent of Samson, such hair suggests energy and magical power. Peter is wrestling with Mark. He is engaging in a magical, playful way with his deceased brother.

By not working in an active profession, Peter finds himself in a situation similar to Mark's before his untimely death. Sloughing off materialism and conventionality, Mark valued creativity, introspection, and relationships—a life to which Peter could not relate at the time. Feelings of guilt overcome Peter. He attempts to write his autobiography, but does not succeed. Finally, he settles into daily work on the many dreams he has each night. This becomes more or less an obsession with him. Through his more serious dream work and stronger connection with the stirrings of his unconscious, Peter's nightly images reach into the collective, archetypal realm. The process begins with a ceremonial odyssey to the land of the dead:

I try to go with my girlfriend to Mark's grave in the cemetery. We're following others who seem to be going on a picnic to their loved one's graves. Obstacles and a sprinkler system in the path keep us from getting there, however. On my second try, my girlfriend joins her friends. I pass a place where baby horses are being birthed. People are helping them. The horses look a bit odd, somewhat like old work horses rather than thoroughbreds.

As in "The Bottom of a Mineshaft" dream that Peter had immediately following Mark's death, he tries to make his way to Mark. In that previous dream, he found himself inside what could be the death tunnel (a mineshaft), but had a difficult time getting there fighting against all of the people coming from the other direction. This time, he tries to make his way to Mark's grave, another death tunnel of sorts, but he is more in tune now with the direction of his psychic energy (everyone is going in the same direction as he is). Peter also has a girlfriend to escort him, one he describes as a motherly type. Peter's nourishing anima attempts to escort him to the place of the dead.

Having lived in Mexico for a short while, Peter is familiar with the yearly celebration of the Day of the Dead. Called *el Dia de los Muertos*, it is celebrated on the second of November, a day when families unite with their dead loved ones in festive celebration at their gravesites. This is also a custom in the Far East, a tradition that brings life and death together each year in ritual celebration. In his dream, Peter tries to attend this special event, but there are still too many obstacles in his way and he is eventually deserted by the feminine aspect that was to take him there.

Peter does not make it to the cemetery, but becomes aware of the birthing place of foals. In many cultures, horses are considered animals of the underworld and are associated with burial rites. The arrival of these young horses intimates the birthing of an instinctual libido within Peter's psyche, a libido that can carry him to the land of the dead or to other realms of consciousness.

Jung tells us that "Legend attributes properties to the horse which psychologically belong to the unconscious of man: there are clairvoyant and clairaudient horses, path-finding horses who show the way when the wanderer is lost, horses with mantic powers. . . . They hear the words the corpse utters on its way to the grave—words which no human can hear."[3] Peter's horses are stocky workhorses, bringing their ancient and work-oriented associations to the task at hand. Perhaps he needs these horses, or libidinal energy, to overcome the obstacles in his path.

Two months later, Peter discovers in a dream "that a part of me I thought dead is still alive." The Mark part? During the following night, when *el Dia de los Muertos* is celebrated in Mexico, Peter discovers a connecting link to this place of death. He titles the dream "The Doorway of Death."

I am at a movie theater. An Italian judge is with me and he has two children with him—his grandchildren, I guess. I go outside and start following some string. Mark comes out and tells me the string leads to death: "It is a doorway to death." I am shocked. I think he says the strands of string are tied to a tree. There are several thin trees growing almost like a wall where he tells me this. It is night outside the movie theater. I am following the string, going to establish if the string belongs to the judge. This movie theater seems to be down near the beach, as are the trees. Right behind them I seem to hear the ocean.

Peter is at a movie theater, a place of projection in which he sees aspects of himself in the everyday world. He is also with an Italian judge. Italians, to Peter "are people who express their emotions freely. Italian judges must have a tough time because they are supposed to be rational and weigh all the facts carefully, but are also human, with strong feelings that must be expressed."

The dream ego is escorted by a rational nature that is also in tune with his feelings. This judging part of Peter has "two grandchildren," implying the wise or senior quality that guides and directs new life. Peter claims that "taking care of his grandchildren is one way the judge can express his feelings freely and in a socially acceptable manner."

Peter steps out into the darkness, or the unconscious, and, with his spontaneously judging guide, finds a string that Mark tells him "leads to death— a doorway to death." He is also told that this string is attached to a tree, which appears to him to be a wall of thin trees that border the ocean. The string connects Peter to trees that portray the doorway to death. They seem like a wall to him that hides the ocean behind it. The ocean is often viewed as the threshold of the universe, eternity, and, within man, the collective unconscious. One can gaze with wonder into its depths, composed of magnificent life forms, jewels, and treasures of past generations.

In Hindu tradition, it is believed that the spiritual thread binds together all things in existence, as a necklace binds together pearls and other treasures of the ocean floor. In Celtic paganism, initiates followed cords that guided them through the darkness of caves and underground temples. Peter is told by Mark that the string he sees leads to "a doorway to death." He is shown the way to the eternal mysteries of life, represented in his dream by the wall of trees and the ocean behind them. Peter wants to establish to whom this string belongs. That very same night, as if in response to his question, he has another dream:

I take the book of which I have a part, and go to see if I can get the complete book at the book-store. I have the incomplete book in a trunk somewhere. This is a book about Thailand—Thai wisdom. This book seems very familiar to me.

Peter has possession of a part of what could be viewed as the Book of Life, represented as a book about the wisdom of Thailand. Thailand's history and character is essentially founded in Buddhism. Monks in their orange robes are seen walking its dirt roads and streets, and the glitter of golden temples is always in sight. In Buddhist tradition, the purpose of life here on Earth is to escape the cycle of rebirth and enter the eternal state of nirvana, or union with the universe. In his dream, Peter knows that he has a part of this ancient culture, or mystery of life, within him. He plans to complete this part of himself by venturing into a bookstore. It is here, in the quiet solitude of words, images, research, and wisdom, that he can find the completeness of his being and the mysteries of existence. In the previous dream, Peter is shown a string that leads to this truth and, in this dream, he knows that he has a part of that truth within him. "This book seems familiar to me," he says.

Two months pass and a profound archetypal dream comes to Peter, one that he titles "Natural Exhibits."

I am at a museum in a dry place like Australia that has the most beautiful natural exhibits I have ever seen. I am overpowered by their originality and beauty. Then I am lowered, along with the woman I am with, into another exhibit and become momentarily trapped. I see a most beautiful exhibit down here of an upside-down ivory tree, its roots up in the air with figures of people—angels—naturally formed in the small, fine roots. My right leg is slightly injured from being scraped on a rock that is part of the exhibit, but even so, I climb right out, to the amazement of the other tourists. A park ranger brings our books out in a basket that he pulls up with a rope. There is a beautiful snake in the basket with the books.

Peter finds himself in a desert-like place, a locale often associated with the underworld. In this place, he's surrounded by "natural exhibits" suggestive of archetypal forms in the collective unconscious. He's on an exploratory journey, it seems, and is lowered to a place of great depth with his female partner.

Peter finds himself trapped down there and his right leg, the conscious and reasoning approach toward life, is momentarily injured. He says it was scraped on one of the rocks in the exhibit, or injured in the descent of his inward journey. His conscious attitude is temporarily wounded, but this is not a problem, because he easily climbs out after his visit down there.

While in the lowest exhibit, Peter sees an amazing sight: an inverted ivory tree, "its roots up in the air, with figures of people—angels—naturally formed in the small, fine roots." This cosmic tree image is well known to Hindus and shamans of Eastern Siberia. It generally appears upside down with its roots in heaven and its foliage on Earth. Jung claims that, for the shamans, "the roots signify hairs and, on the trunk, near the roots, a face has been carved, showing that the tree represents man"—an image of the shaman himself and his greater personality. "The shaman climbs the magic tree in order to find his true self in the upper world," a mystical experience that is necessary in the search for your true nature.[4]

Following is a quote from the *Bhagavad-Gita*, the famous book of India's spiritual wisdom and guide to the science of self-realization:

> . . . It is said that there is an imperishable Banyan tree that has its roots upward and its branches down and whose leaves are the Vedic hymns. One who knows this tree is the knower of the Vedas.[5]

Bhaktivedanta Swami Prabhupada says you must know this tree through analytical study in order to obtain Christ, or universal consciousness. The tree (or man) of the material world is only a reflection of the real tree in the spiritual world. It is like the reflection one sees in a lake—the upside down tree is an exact replica of the Tree of Life. The reflection is not real and it can come and go depending upon the circumstances. However, the original tree is eternal. In the branches are manifestations of living entities—the lower branches contain lower life forms and the higher branches, or roots of the tree, contain higher life forms such as demigods and angels. "The Banyan tree (Ashvattha) is one of the highest and most beautiful trees, and people in India often worship it as one of their daily morning rituals."[6] The Tree of Life is also worshipped in Western society in the form of the Christmas tree.

Jung sees the image of the Tree of Life as a projection of the individuation process, which he refers to as "an inner process of development independent of the conscious will."[7] When awareness of the Self becomes active, the eternal or angelic realm associated with the heavens, or essence of the Self, becomes concretized. This Peter perceives while in the depths of his psyche. He says: "There is something very permanent about the ivory quality of the root system, yet it can be destroyed too, I think." Peter senses that the permanency of the heavens within can be destroyed by wrong living and an outer orientation to life.

The injury to Peter's right leg does not keep him from returning to the outer world and bringing his newly gained knowledge with him. He climbs out, to the amazement of everyone, and a ranger pulls up his books, along with a snake. "It's a beautiful snake," Peter says, "maybe two feet long and as round as an ordinary garden hose, with bright bands of red, green, yellow, and blue."

As in the Gilgamesh epic, Peter's psyche has journeyed into what can be viewed as the abode of the dead or the nether regions. At the end of his journey, Gilgamesh brings up the herb of life that he harvested in the depths of the water. He says: "This plant is a wondrous plant, Whereby a man may obtain his former strength."[8] Gilgamesh was not destined to take the plant back with him, however. On his journey home, the plant of renewed life is snatched by a serpent and taken back into the depths of the water, along with the immortality that Gilgamesh so desperately sought.

In Peter's dream, a serpent of wondrous beauty is brought up with his books. He says it contains bands of red, green, yellow, and blue, suggestive of fire and heat, vegetation and healing, wisdom and intuition, and eternity. As with Gilgamesh, Peter did not take home the Tree or herb of Life, but he did find it. Gilgamesh was deeply affected by his journey into the underworld and by the serpent; he became a better and more dependable king upon his return. This transformation is possible for Peter, too, who has experienced, inwardly, the archetype of renewed life. Peter reclaims the books that he carried down and that were brought back up from the depths of his being. These books may very well be his life's work. They could represent the dream work he so devotedly attends to each day, and they may represent Peter's personal Book of Life.

Two months pass and Peter has a dream:

"Where's Mark, Peter?" a little girl asks me in an auditorium full of praying people.
"He's in the war."
"How did Mark die, Peter?"
"A bomb blew up. Pray for him."

Mark's death is a tragic loss to Peter, and he knows he must pray for him. When you pray, you put forth full attention and libido on the image of God and the depths of the unconscious, the place of God within. Peter is reminded that the Mark aspect of him is gone. It blew up sometime in his past and should now become the focus of his attention. He's reminded to maintain prayerful focus on Mark, which could ultimately save his life.

Several months later, Peter is again shown the lack of Mark-ness in his life through the following dream:

I have no shirt on and this makes me feel uncomfortable. Later, along with brother, Robert, I am looking for something to eat. Robert is talking and shouting to himself in this office room while I observe as a distant stranger. I seem to be living in this place because Mark is dead. A very pretty girl shows me her teeth and asks me if I think she drinks. I hesitate to answer, see how nice her skin is, and say "no." She says I am right. Then she gives me a ride and there is another, a black girl, in our car that is headed toward this temporary place where I am staying after Mark's funeral/death. I am very interested in this black girl (her friend?), but, due to Mark's death, it isn't appropriate to do anything with her.

Peter is exposed emotionally (wears no shirt) and is uncomfortable because of it. He is also hungry for nourishment, while the Robert part of him (the part with no spiritual connection) is angry. Peter witnesses this movie-like dilemma as he stands apart and observes, then realizes that he is in this place because "Mark is dead"—that living, breathing soul aspect of his nature is gone.

As often happens in dreams, Peter is shown a way out of this lifelong predicament. With the help of a young, radiant anima figure, who is level-headed and does not drink, he is taken toward the temporary place of grief and death. On his way, he sees a black girl with whom he would like to con-nect. Peter says: "I would like to have sexual intercourse with her, to merge with her feminine energy, but it seems sacrilegious or dangerous to do some-thing like that so close to Mark's death. I also feel that I have to maintain my masculine 'toughness' so I won't show my real (soft) feelings to Robert, who is angry."

Peter remembers how Robert ridiculed his soft side, his sensitivity and feelings, in childhood. By responding sensitively to his feelings and spiritual life now, Peter fears the loss of Robert's love, the one person left who is like a father to him. Uniting with the blackness of his feminine soul is difficult for Peter, but he does not completely turn her away. Instead he says: "The time is not quite right yet."

Black images in dreams usually represent the initial, or primal, stage of a psychological process. Like the Dark Night of the Soul, black is the "descent into hell." It is the state of fermentation and decomposition, of being hidden from view and, essentially, in darkness. Peter's dream contains two women—one white, one black—the duality of opposites in nature and a powerful force in the individuation process. They act as a team that drives him to the place of death, where his transformative image of Mark awaits him. It is still too soon for Peter, however. He must first release the ties from those he feels he needs.

Not long after this dream, Peter and Robert have a "big falling out." Peter stops trying to get Robert's approval for the way he has chosen to live his life, one quite different from the life Robert lives. This act alone releases a lot of pent-up energy for him. Peter is now able to make an effort to meet like-minded people. He joins a dream organization and a dream group. At one of the meetings, he works intensely on a dream that ultimately frees him from the survivor's guilt he has been carrying. Shortly after this meeting, the following dream comes to him:

While at an art gallery, I pick up a black girl with big boobs. I try to make it with her several times, but we are always interrupted. Then we go somewhere with a bunch of guys I knew from high school. We stop in a store that sells model airplanes and I'm shown a pair of fold-up shoes that are no longer in fashion. After I put the shoes down, I notice Mark standing there. He tells me about the many "babes" living in the part of town where he is now living. This black babe that I have picked up seems crazy about sex, out of control. She participates in a lot of sex, but feels nothing in her sex organs.

Sex in dreams usually represents an intimate interaction with an aspect of one's nature, often shown as an archetypal image. Here, it is the dark, multi-breasted Earth Mother, goddess of death and nourisher of life. Peter picks up, or seduces, this black woman in a place suggestive of the dream world, an art gallery. Mark, the supporter in Peter's union with the feminine, again appears to him at this significant moment. By telling Peter about the "many babes living in the part of town where he is now living," he associates his relationship with the black girl to that profound place of life beyond death.

Peter's dreams suggest that he is heavily involved in inner work, but, because of the many distractions from an immature, masculine nature, he is still not able to unite fully with his anima soul. His adolescent-acting masculinity takes him to a flighty place (a store that sells model airplanes). Peter puts up with this way of being, but suddenly realizes that the shoes, or his life stance brought on by this attitude, are out of fashion and can be folded up and put away. Peter does, indeed, put the shoes away. Then, as an apparent consequence, Mark arrives to remind him of the seductive possibilities that are awaiting him in the darkness of the underworld. The moment is very hot and ripe for him.

Returning to the beginning of Peter's process, we find that he had a significant sacred prostitute dream immediately following Mark's death. In the dream, he was invited by a princess to have sex with her as part of a ritual celebration, but was told by a wise source that this wouldn't work because of his "attitude problem." That strong proclamation affected Peter to the core and, as a result, he decided to take himself more seriously. Peter worked even more intensely with his dreams, quit his job to rebalance his outer life, and tended to his alcohol and drug dependence. Through his commitment to grow and deepen spiritually, Peter does, indeed, arrive at a new soul place. He appears quite ready this time to unite with the dark sacredness that the prostitute represents, and she is certainly energized and seductive.

Shortly after this dream, Peter begins analysis and continues working with his dreams with the guidance and support of that relationship. Mark appears in his dreams during this time mostly as a soul mate. They play together as they never did in childhood and a union forms between them. They share emotions, explore the archetypal world of the collective, and play again like children. In one dream sequence, they wrestle playfully as their mother watches in approval; in another, they share a pleasurable moment of junk food. In yet another dream, they look with amazement at a branch of birds floating through the air, something that can happen only in the spaceless dimension of the dream world. Their togetherness is then consummated in a dream that Peter has, not once, but several times:

Mark and I are in bed together, making slow love while we talk about things going on in the family. The question seems to be who is going to do what to whom, although I have the feeling that he has more experience in this sort of thing than I do.

Peter has come to a new relationship and a union with his inner secret world, the world that Mark knows and now inhabits. He wonders who should be the initiator in this relationship and senses that it should be Mark, the one who resides in and represents that soul place. He dreams:

I'm staying with Mark, his wife, and their new baby. There is a dark Indonesian girl there who wants to make love with me. She kisses me and tells me "You know what I want." Later, Mark silently holds up a condom for me to see. I nod. The girl and I—all of us?—are resting on a mattress on the floor.

Peter and Mark have certainly become partners in their soul journey. Because of Peter's courage in facing his weaknesses and fears, he is now in a better condition psychologically to consummate his relationship with his feminine soul. In the end, Mark's home, Peter's inner room, is filled with family and new life. Mark guides Peter in his union with the sacred prostitute, and they all lie together on one giant mattress, the place of sleep and dreams.

The next day, Peter hears a phrase while in deep sleep: "We hope you will take over for Mark. Do his work. Mark had a rich, inner life." Peter's continuous reminders of Mark's rich inner life and secret inner room are "soul callings" that demand to be lived. James Hillman states: "A calling may be postponed, avoided, intermittently missed. It may also possess you completely. Whatever; eventually it will out. It makes its claim. The daemon does not go away."[9]

What exactly is "Mark's rich, inner life," to Peter? Peter reminisces about Mark and their lifetime together: "I think we were both pretty sensitive, but we tried to act very macho so that no one would know; and because of our sensitivity, I'm sure there were times we felt very vulnerable and exposed. We liked beautiful people and beautiful things, and we were kind and generous in a way. Mostly, however, we were dreamers and interested in spiritual things, but were usually embarrassed to admit it and often made fun of my mother for her interest in such matters.

"Mark's death has played a huge role in turning my life around. I was living a pretty unhappy, unconscious, materialistic existence until he died. Seeing him die and realizing how tenuous life is made me realize that I had better start living the kind of life I want to live rather than the kind of life others wanted until it was too late. As I look back at Mark's life, I realize that he lived most of his life on his terms in spite of the rest of us. I can now see that Mark's life was an inspiration to me. I can be gentle, kind, humorous, vulnerable, and relatively free like he was. I can just 'be' rather than having to be doing something all the time. I can also have a spiritual existence without the world coming down on me."

Taking the matter of change to heart, Peter ponders what he has been through over the past five years. He considers the unbearable grief of losing a brother who was dear to him, the difficulty of working in a profession that seemed futile, and his escape from the reality of it through drug and alcohol use. He ponders his dream life and the work he has done with those dreams. Then he reviews what he has now:

"I am much less afraid of life, living, death, other people and of what is going on inside of me. At the same time, I am more vulnerable and in touch with the frightened child inside of me. I am less materialistic than I was before, living my life more on my terms, more consciously. I know that I am more tolerant, compassionate and patient with myself and others. Definitely, I am more reflective. I feel like a student trying to learn as much as I can about what it is to live a whole life, a life that includes spiritual elements. I never gave this any thought until a few years ago. Working with my dreams on a daily basis helps me to keep my attitudes in balance and shows me where I still have work to do."

Through the image of his union with the dark feminine, Peter knows that he has entered that dark soul place of dreams. Through the image of the Tree of Life, he has experienced the depths of the soul's union with that transcendental place called the heavens. Peter's life in the outer world has also changed in the work that he does, as well as in his ability to relate on a more emotional level with those who are special to him.

Peter dreams:

I am in a conversation with an old woman who has seen her husband die a long time ago because of his ambition. We are holding hands and sitting on the grass as we talk. I tell her that I have no ego—that I wish I had more ego.

"You will live longer," she says.

"Yes, I can tell people, if they ask, that what I am doing is living longer."

She and I seem pretty pleased with this idea. I have been talking to her at a small private school that I am visiting and then we have to leave because it is 5:00 P.M. and the school is closing. I am with Mark, looking for the car to go home.

The old woman seems disgusted with ambitious men and their egos—their constant need to prove themselves. Her son, an ambitious man, a builder, has been standing off in the distance. He waves goodbye.

Part Three

CELEBRATING DEATH

chapter eight

HOLIDAY FOR THE DEAD—
EL DIA DE LOS MUERTOS

In the transient realm of time and space, there is constant change, or cessation, in form and expression; but the essence within these changes endures. Everlasting is the soul of man (the true Self) and the soul of the universe . . . the "thou and I" expressions of Spirit.

—PARAMAHANSA YOGANANDA, *The Bhagavad Gita*

During the last week of October, the people of Mexico prepare for one of their most important annual celebrations—*el Dia de los Muertos*, the Day of the Dead. Outdoor markets specific to this occasion appear with their *cempasuchi*, the marigold-like flower of the season, yard-long incense candles, ceramics and candies in the shape of skeletons and skulls, bread for the dead, and other items prepared for home altars and graves. Since ancient times, our southern neighbors have believed that early fall is when the boundary between life and death becomes permeable, allowing the souls of the living and dead to commune. In Western countries, Halloween is a carryover of this tradition, although it is only a semblance of this profoundly spiritual celebration of the Day of the Dead. Celebrated in all regions of Mexico in one form or another, this holiday has evolved from the beliefs of the indigenous people combined with the Roman Catholicism brought by the Spaniards.

The celebrants believe that death transcends boundaries and expands upon and becomes intermingled with life on Earth. Those who have died live in another realm, where they serve as a link between God and their loved ones who still live on the material plane. Children are taught early about death and how to respect and value the continued relationship they have with their ancestors. They play a key role in these ceremonies.

On October 28, thoughts turn to those who have died and the rituals begin. Young children don costumes of skeletons, witches, ghouls, and devils, and dance in the streets. Some groups carry caskets, as if in a funeral procession. The occasion is not solemn, but gay, with a carnival-like atmosphere. The purpose is clearly to celebrate the dead and the relationship they have with them. In the homes, large, wall-sized altars are constructed for the dead souls who will visit. They are made with objects from the ancient cultures. Arches of reed or cornhusks are built high above the altars, in a shape that symbolizes time, the cycle of death and resurrection, and the union between those on Earth and those who have died. Cempasuchi flowers, the flower of the dead, cover the arch. A relative of the marigold, this flower grows abundantly in Mexico at this time of year. It has had great religious significance among the ancient people and is regarded as a symbol of wisdom, beauty, truth, and eternity. By offering flowers of any kind, one pays homage to the deceased's virtues and forgets any hatred or angry feelings that may have been a part of the relationship.

Once the basic structure of the altar is prepared, it is decorated with food and drink for the expected visitors, including fruit and nuts, hot chocolate, mezcal, tobacco, candy skulls, and bread made specially for the occasion. Pictures of the deceased and their favorite articles and toys are also included. Incense from the resin of the copal tree is burned in a three-legged vessel that represents the three means of communicating with the gods and the three elements through which the souls come to them: the firmament, the earth, and the air. Candles are lit to help the souls find their way home. It is believed that, on these days consecrated to them, the dead join their loved ones through the light of the candle and the aroma of their favorite foods.

On October 31, the souls of dead children, or *angelitos*, are venerated. Midday, church bells toll and, in some villages, may continue tolling all day and night until sunset of November 2, when the souls go back to the realm of the dead. In the early morning hours of November 1, families congregate in full celebration at the cemeteries of the cities, towns, and pueblos. Small groups unite around their family gravesites with armloads of flowers and bundles of yard-long candles to place in and around each grave. They then sit quietly and respectfully, wrapped warmly in blankets, and share stories of the deceased and their times together. The atmosphere is filled with music and laughter, or it may be quietly contemplative and meditative. Each family has its unique experience and each is respected. The aura of spirituality and union is so intense at this time that you can feel the presence of the dead souls in the air. It is not frightening; it is a moment of awe, wonder, and profound beauty. As one villager says: "To see all the lights, we know they have arrived."

THREE DAYS WITH THE DEAD

Not long ago, I had an opportunity to participate in the ceremony and rituals of *el Dia de los Muertos* near the lovely city of Oaxaca, in southern Mexico. With a group of eight, we were guided by two spiritualists through the ritual of worshipping our deceased loved ones and reconnecting with them. Our three-day ritual began with the preparation of an altar—"our altar," as we called it. On the altar, we arranged fruit, nuts, candies, bread, flowers, and candles in patterns that spoke to each of us. Then we placed pictures of, or objects special to, our deceased loved ones. In the center, I placed pictures of my son, Michael, and my mother, who had died fifteen months before. The next day, one of our spiritualist guides made a cross of lime powder on the floor in front of the altar. Four candles were placed on each end of the cross and the area was sprinkled with cempasuchi petals. We were told that the lime attracts the souls, as do the candles and the favorite foods and special objects of the deceased. A second spiritualist sang songs to the deceased and we prayed for them to come to us.

Later in the evening, our small group gathered in front of the altar to talk about our loved ones—how they died, happy and sad memories of our lives with them, and the meaning of life and death to us. I felt immersed in thoughts of Michael, the prophecies surrounding his death, the torment I experienced with my family and friends at the hospital, and how he has returned to me in my dreams through the years. This, I shared. I also heard the stories of my fellow group members as they, too, experienced their loved ones passing from life into the realm of death. We parted with deep emotion that night, feeling the profound wonder of the moment.

The next morning, I was flooded with a series of dreams, feeling that death had again filled my psyche. One dream dramatized my son's return to the Earth, another addressed the dynamic interconnectedness of life and death. In the first dream of my son:

I hear a legend-like prophecy that someone has given birth to a child. This child seems to be my son. Years pass and I have forgotten that he is someone very special to me. Then I'm in a small womb-like boat and a storm strikes. It seems as if I know in advance that this storm will come to pass, but I had forgotten this, too. It hits violently and submerges the boat. I feel myself going under the water and believe I am going to drown, but I manage to hold my breath until I am projected back up to the surface. Somewhere at the bottom is my son.

Later, a young child comes to me and I know he was my son at one time. He gives me a big hug and I feed him. I tell my husband that I just saw our son. "How could we have forgotten that he is our son?" I say in agony.

The theory of reincarnation has been an aspect of most religions throughout the world, including early Christianity. It is especially widespread in the Hindu and Buddhist traditions of the East. Even in Western society today, famous philosophers and scholars believe in reincarnation and often include it in their writings. Literature is rich with the stories and testimonies of those, many of them children under the age of seven, who remember living previous lives.

Tibetan Buddhists traditionally recognize and search for what they call *tulkus*, or incarnations of their spiritual leaders. This tradition began in the 13th century and continues today. Spiritual disciples and friends of deceased lamas often have dreams that foretell the fact and location of their rebirth. The purpose of searching for these spiritual souls is to awaken the wisdom memory within the new incarnations so it may be continued without interruption.[1] Often, the children they find have a remarkable knowledge of the Buddhist tradition at a very early age, even when not born in the East. Sogyal Rinpoche claims that a tulku is not the exact same person he was in his previous incarnation. She or he may have the same spirit and motivation toward life, talents and knowledge, but be a very different person with completely different life experiences.

Why does my dream indicate that my son has returned and that I have forgotten that this would come to pass? Why is anyone, including the Buddhists, shown this fact in a dream? I have seen instances of possible reincarnations in some of the dream series that I have explored, which suggests to me that this is not unusual. Your dreams contain all earthly and spiritual possibilities, from the beginning of time and into the future. Dreams are not exclusive, but contain all of what life, death, and afterlife involves. If reincarnation is an aspect of your continuing development as souls, then that too will be a part of your dreams.

In my dream, I hear this prophecy and suffer a tragedy in my life. Did I not have a premonition of my son's approaching death? As ordained, the life vessel in which I live sinks into the depths of darkness. I become submerged in it and rise back to the surface, as if reborn. The experience is a death-rebirth process, one that I did, indeed, experience through the death of my son. Then I realize that I have forgotten that life does proceed from one birth into another. It plays to the possibility that my son is back on Earth and that, someday, I may meet him or her. The significance of this message to me is that I must not forget the soul of my son; I must be ready to "feed" or nurture him or her if and when the time comes to do so. Perhaps someday, I may have to teach or give to this child in a way I was not able to do as its mother.

In the second dream that night:

I have returned to my tropical fish tank and find that one large, dark oblong fish has died. I stand above the tank on a ladder and try to scoop the dead fish out with a net, but am unable to do so because the many living fish end up in the net with it. I am unable to differentiate between the dead fish and the living fish. They cannot be separated. Feeling frustrated, I hop off the ladder and discover that there is another tank of fish right underneath the one in which I was working. It is quite dark, not unlike a tomb under the ground.

Fish symbolize many things, including life and fertility, sexuality, Christ the savior, and resurrection and immortality. Since I am, at this time, heavily immersed in issues of death and immortality through the Day of the Dead experience, the fish in my dream are suggestive of resurrection and immortality. There are many ancient myths that incorporate fish as a symbol of immortality and rebirthing, as well as of the process of transformation leading toward psychic wholeness. In ancient Greece, it was believed that the souls of the dead could be reborn by becoming fish. In Christian teachings, fish in a net represent the faithful in the waters of life hoping for immortality. In ancient Egypt, fish represent the soul nature of man and the unborn child. When you fish within yourself, you extract unconscious elements from the deep place of wisdom. Fish are the essence of soul matter, because they live in the regenerative water of life.

In the dream, I am trying to net an amorphous black blob that I know is the remains of a fish. The fish is oblong, lacking bones and skin. In alchemy, such a fish is considered the "round element," or the essential nature of the Self. It is impossible for me to separate this essential element from the life within the tank. They seem as one. Then I discover that below this world is another, very dark, unknown world. Jung says: "From the negredo [darkness] issues the Stone, the symbol of the immortal Self; moreover, its first appearance is likened to 'fish eyes'." [2] This lower fish tank contains the unknown mysteries of life, that which is the nourishing influence for the actively living world above it. As Jung claims: "Consciousness does not produce its energy by itself." [3] In this dream, my dream ego becomes involved with the basic mystery and essence of life, death, consciousness, and immortality. It contains no answers, but does show that there is a profound mystery of life that you are unable to see on the surface of things. Through your conscious relatedness to death, you may find that essential reality and source of life itself and come into close communion with it.

Shortly after midnight on the morning of November 1, I enter the small pueblo cemetery hidden behind a row of shacks and houses of tin and adobe. A gateway divides the cemetery from the houses that camouflage it. I am surprised to see that the cemetery is quiet. The hordes of people I anticipate haven't yet arrived. Instead, a quiet group of peasant women sits to the right, just inside the entrance, laughing and socializing quietly while cooking up vats of hot drinks for the anticipated event. On the left side of the gate sit their men, the elders and leaders of the pueblo.

"So simple," I think to myself as I walk among the mounds of dirt, some marked with decorative metal crosses and others unmarked. Intermingled among these simple grave mounds are more elaborate cement structures, possibly the graves of those whose families have the financial resources to have them built. To explore the cemetery, I am forced to wander in the blackness of the night, because someone said it is disrespectful to use a flashlight. I want to honor their customs and show respect for their dead. Stumbling among graves placed in random fashion, I think of how very different this cemetery is from the one in which my son is buried. I am not even allowed to plant flowers on his grave because of the rigid standards that allow for only a cement slab marker embedded in grass to mark his place. The flowers I put in a container provided by the cemetery are removed each week so the lawn can be cut. It certainly isn't a place where you can maintain a heart-felt memorial to your loved ones.

Several families have already arrived at the pueblo cemetery and have decorated their loved ones' graves with flowers and candles. I am touched with sadness when I see a young man and his young boy placing purple long-stemmed irises on what appears to be a fresh grave. They then tenderly outline the grave with yard-long candles and quietly sit beside it. I wonder if the man is decorating the grave of his young wife and the boy's mother who may have recently died. In quiet solemnity, they sit in the dim darkness, lighted only by the radiant candles. Later that night, I see the boy sleeping on the ground beside the grave, snuggled warmly in a blanket, with his father sitting beside him.

"What dreams this boy will have tonight!" I think. Possibly, his mother will come to visit and tell him how much she loves and misses him. She may come as an angel, affirming that she is still with him, even though in another realm. He will be comforted by her and know that life does have meaning and purpose in spite of his tragic loss.

I make my way back to the entrance and am met by a troupe of villagers carrying trumpets, trombones, saxophones, guitars, and drums. They sit quietly near the entrance and play their first song of the night, a popular Mexican birthday song. The festivities begin. It is two o'clock in the morning. Family upon family parade through the entrance, each carrying bundles of flowers and candles in their arms, on their heads, and in wheelbarrows, and— baskets filled with food and drink, radios. They come to celebrate—and celebrate heartily. Their energy and enthusiasm is high. Slowly, the cemetery fills with radiant light from the candles as each grave is decorated with carpets of flowers and candles of the dead. Not one grave is missed.

Once the plots are decorated, the families sit around them, sharing stories of times past, memories of the deceased, and hopes of times to come. Some groups play their own special music, while the band plays in the distance. I'm impressed at how each family is able to celebrate without intruding upon or being bothered by another, even in such close quarters. The music they play appears to be absorbed by the atmosphere, as if transmitted immediately into the realm of the dead. So quiet, yet so festive. Certainly, I have never experienced such a moving sight before. The peacefulness surrounds me, as if I were indeed among the dead and they with me. Standing here, I feel as though I am in another place and time—that I am, indeed, in that place called liminality.

Daylight slowly creeps over the cemetery, bringing the festivities at the gravesites to a peaceful close. Families gather their belongings and return home to a celebratory breakfast of *pan de muerto* (bread of the dead), hot chocolate, tortillas, *huevos rancheros*, and other favorites.

November first, All Soul's Day, is also called "The Grand Day" in Oaxaca. It is believed that God and all the souls of the deceased come to Earth at noon to be with the living. Many remain beside their altars, recollect, and go within on this day. In the evening, villagers may don costumes representing the dead and other dark characters, and dance robustly in the streets. Instinctively, they know that, with God and the dead souls, comes darkness and evil—that they cannot be separated. The only way to relate to a force as powerful as the dark side of God is to mimic, to dance and act it out, so that the force cannot take control. The indigenous people of Mexico, and other ancient cultures of the world, know how to relate to such powerful forces. They do not deny them or pretend that God is only goodness and light. They express His darkness through ritual and ceremony in a safe and contained place within the confines of their village.

The Day of the Dead is a season of transformation. Not only do the dead souls return to the material world, but the dead within us also rises. As in my dream prior to the Day of the Dead, I become submerged under the water when my ship of life sinks into the depths. I remain there as long as I can, a time that seems endless, and return to the light of the surface. The dead within me has arisen to face a new beginning, a new birth. Not only has my son returned to me, but I too have arisen.

On the morning after my experience at the cemetery, I dream:

I'm back at the cemetery with an unknown presence who guides me by the hand in the darkness between the graves. I hear the words el medio, *and know that this is a problem that must be overcome—that I must stay in the middle as I walk among the graves. I know that this is not an individual, but a universal problem that all of mankind must confront. Nearby, I see a woman from our group holding her baby in her arms. She is a strong presence within the setting of the dark cemetery.*

The middle, or center space, is the boundary between the two worlds of time/space and timelessness/spacelessness. It is the void of liminality to which death takes you, whether you go there through a physical death or experience a death, rebirth, and resurrection process within yourself. In the dream, I am guided through the middle or center space and the problem is pointed out to me—that I must walk this fine line, or be fully aware of it, when communing with the world of the dead. There are several inferences here. The first is that there must be a firm boundary between the living and the dead. You can relate to that realm at certain times and in specific circumstances, but should never become enmeshed in it. Being obsessed by the dead can lead to potential psychological problems. "The problem is *el medio*, to remain in the middle," wise words say to me. The second inference points to the transformative potential inherent in walking the middle ground, or center space. Since a mother and her newborn baby are a strong presence near the center space, this second point speaks most to me, although both appear to be true.

In the dream, I stumble in the darkness of what seems to be a forest as well as a cemetery. The setting is similar to a cave-like place of incubation and darkness. Jung states:

> Anyone who gets into that cave, that is to say into the cave which everyone has in himself, or into the darkness that lies behind consciousness, will find himself involved in an—at first—unconscious process of transformation. By penetrating into the unconscious he makes a connection with his unconscious contents. This may result in a momentous change of personality in the positive or negative sense. The transformation is often interpreted as a prolongation of the natural span of life or an earnest [glimpse] of immortality.[4]

For one night, I have lived in that timeless-spaceless place of liminality and death, and return from it with a vague sense of having been reborn. My fellow seminarians say that I am different—more outgoing and engaged with them. Internally, I feel more confident and in tune with the order of things as they are on Earth. Perhaps through my recognition, prayers, and love to a world beyond what I know, I have communed with the dimension of the lower fish tank in my earlier dream, that essential reality and the regenerative water of life itself.

chapter nine

YOUR BEREAVEMENT DREAM SANCTUARY

Even in our sleep
Pain which cannot forget
Falls drop by drop upon the heart,
Until in our own despair
Against our will
Comes wisdom,
To the awful grace of God.

—AESCHYLUS, *The Oresteia*

"Often my mother comes to me at night in my dreams," Francesca, one of the spiritualists in our seminar group, says. "We were very close when she was alive, so when she died, I thought I would not be able to go on. Suddenly, she began appearing to me in my dreams. She guides me almost daily now, as if we have never parted. When I have a problem, before I go to sleep, I ask her to help me with it, and then she comes."

Francesca participated with my group at the *Dia de los Muertos* workshop in Oaxaca. When she shared this on our first night together, I felt skeptical about her dependency on the spirit of her mother. My customary Western view takes such dependency with a large dose of skepticism. Is this healthy?

We're supposed to be strong and go on with life after a loss—not be tied to the ghosts of our loved ones forever!

One week with Francesca, however, helped me to see that she was quite healthy mentally, and even wise in her own way. An indigenous woman living in a third-world country, she was independent, capable, and highly respected by her peers. She understood in many ways how to find true guidance and wisdom through an intimate connection with her soul. Cultures such as hers have experience and knowledge in the ways of the spirit world that embody thousands of years of history. They also know when not to intrude upon it. I suspect that the image of Francesca's mother in her dreams was Francesca's own motherly wisdom, rather than the actual soul of her mother, and that, at some level, she knew that. Five years had passed since her mother's death. It is doubtful that her soul would have remained so long on the earthly plane, or that the mother would have encouraged such a dependent relationship with her daughter. Of significance in Francesca's story is the open and attentive relationship she had with the divine wisdom within, and how this wisdom revealed itself through the loving image of her mother.

As is typical in Hispanic and many other cultures throughout the world, Francesca was using a technique that is often referred to as "dream incubation." Calling out directly to her mother for a dream made the process a more personal one for her. Hebrews refer to dream incubation as *she'elat chalom*, which literally means "dream question."[1] More specifically, it is a pre-sleep preparation for receiving a dream. Temples in ancient Mesopotamia that date back to 3000 B.C. were constructed just for that purpose—to bring soul guidance and physical and emotional healing to those who suffered through a form of dream incubation.

Dreams are a tool to use during difficult times if you trust in the wisdom and guidance that can come from them. This is especially so when you are grieving. Dreams come to you whether you ask for them or not, but to use them as guidance is another matter. In the four dream stories in this book, some dreamers worked diligently with their dreams, while others barely recorded them. In my own case, for example, I recorded my dreams primarily out of curiosity during the years immediately following Michael's death. I had little connection with the wisdom that they contained. It wasn't until much later that I had the opportunity to work with these dreams through my personal analysis. Then, and only then, did I engage with the images that the dreams revealed to me, and through that divine work, was finally able to come to terms with the tragic loss I had suffered.

Bereavement is a painful process that can continue for many years. Some don't have the energy or even the desire to go beyond it, while others may feel helplessly trapped in their suffering and long to find a way through it. In these cases, specific rituals, like creating an altar, prayer and meditation, dream incubation, journaling, and dream tending, may help. I call these rituals a "bereavement dream sanctuary," because of their sacredness and intentionality to the process of healing.

THE HOME ALTAR

Westerners, particularly those in the United States, need a private place for their departed loved ones. Over the years, many cemeteries have become cold and barren places that don't invite quiet contemplation or spiritual dialog. Compare Western cemeteries to those in other parts of the world—cemeteries filled with mementos, flowers, and candles perpetually glowing in memory of those buried there. We don't realize what we have lost in our pursuit of a clean and efficient environment until we see how other cultures honor their dead. During my years as a student in Switzerland, I often walked through the cemetery in the little town of Küsnacht for the peace and solitude it offered. It was truly an inviting place, filled with the memories of generations of loved ones, most buried in family plots. I walked among the tombstones, read stories of lives past, and took in the aura of love and devotion that filled each grave. Cemeteries there are sacred places, and each grave has the appearance of an altar in memory of that precious loved one whose remains lie buried beneath it.

Cemeteries in Mexico are much simpler and somewhat rustic in appearance, but come vibrantly alive during the season of el Dia de los Muertos. Catholicism, with a strong mix of ancient spiritualism, dominates their culture. One can easily see this during the season of the dead, as well as in their homes, where many families have an altar in a corner in memory of their departed family members. It is here, at the altar site, where their loved ones' special possessions, photos, flowers, and candles of devotion are placed. Within their homes, they can easily stop to say a prayer or speak privately with a loved one with little intrusion from the outside world. It is here that true grieving occurs.

I suggest that you create an altar in your home for your recently departed, or for a loved one for whom you continue to grieve. The altar can be as simple as a photo on a small table with a candle or flower beside it, or as grand as you feel it should be. Some of the altars in Mexico cover an entire wall. Express yourself as freely as you choose with whatever memories, crafts, artifacts, and items of devotion bring to your mind special moments with your loved one. This is your private space and your expression of the one you loved. Here, in the privacy of your home, you can sit, speak to your loved one, pray, and meditate.

The altar is a place for privacy as well as for family gatherings. What better place to invite your children when a family member has died? By including children in your grief and ritual process, they too will bring resolution to the pain of loss. If not, depression and an essentially unlived life can haunt them well through adulthood. Judy Tatelbaum claims: "Many of us fear that if allowed in, grief will bowl us over indefinitely. The truth is that grief experienced does dissolve. The only grief that does not end is grief that has not been fully faced. Grief unexpressed is like a powder keg waiting to be ignited."[2]

You can bring closure to a loss at your altar and through the rituals you do. In Mexico, children are included in all activities and rituals of their Day of the Dead celebration. From early on, they know death so intimately that they learn to play with it. You can do this with your children as well. Communicate to them that death is a part of life and that it is not an absolute end to the love and memory of their cherished one. Through your rituals, they too will learn the transformative power of grieving and letting go.

PRAYER AND MEDITATION

Many cultures and religions affirm that prayer and meditation are the most effective ways to relieve the pain of grief. Praying to a departed loved one honors their memory, lets them know (even if gone from sight) that they are loved and missed, and eases the pain that you both are experiencing.

Sogyal Rinpoche claims that the deceased can suffer as much grief and agony over their death as their surviving loved ones. This may be especially pronounced if the death occurred suddenly or tragically. The Tibetans claim that the first forty-nine days of the bardo of becoming, immediately following the death, is the most crucial time to help them. It is then that their spirits are closest to the material plane. With sudden deaths, some souls may not be aware of their changed existence and may linger in a frantic state trying to get the attention of their loved ones. Prayers for them and respectful awareness of the possible presence of their souls at this delicate time can alleviate their suffering, as well as your own. In Tibet, these first forty-nine days are also considered a critical period for the bereaved. Family and community members traditionally remain nearby until the time has passed. Not until after the forty-nine days are they encouraged to return to daily life. How different this is from our Western orientation, with its three days of funeral leave.

Some of the greatest pain you suffer comes from a feeling that you are completely severed from helping or connecting with the one you've lost. There are ways, however, that you can give to and join with your loved one. Prayer, encouraged by many spiritual traditions, is one of them. Prayer is not only important immediately following the death, but for many years after. To pray most productively, set aside a period to be with your loved one in front of the altar you've prepared. Quietly take in the essence of your loved one's presence, imagine a warm, healing light surrounding him or her, and talk or cry in the language of your heart. To pray like this is one of the most healing and powerful things you can do for yourself, as well as for your departed loved one. Sogyal Rinpoche states, "Be confident that if someone you love very much has died, and you pray for them with true love and sincerity, your prayer will be exceptionally powerful."[3] Speak to her or him in the words and emotions that are true to you. You may feel love, sadness, agony, guilt, or anger. Allow the feelings to permeate your being for as long as necessary, then let yourself feel refreshed and cleansed from their release.

After praying, continue to sit, with your attention focused inward, in a meditative state. Sit with your feet flat on the floor, spine erect, hands loosely relaxed in your lap, and eyes focused either at the point between your eyebrows or toward your heart. Such a pose allows for the emotional and spiritual energy to flow unimpeded through your body and out your head chakra. You may sit on a straight-backed chair or on the floor with your legs crossed. Do whatever feels most comfortable for you. Remain in this pose for as long as you can, while absorbing the essence of your being, your thoughts, and any other emotion that may flow through you.

DREAM INCUBATION

Dream incubation has been practiced by many cultures, including the Christians and Jews, for thousands of years. The tradition of dream incubation closest to our Western culture is that of the Greek healer, Aesculapius. The word "incubation" in Greek is *enkoimesis*, which means "sleeping in the sanctuary."

In recent times, there has been a renewed interest in this effective method of seeking wisdom from within, with some research on its results. In a 1993 study, subjects from a university setting were instructed to incubate a dream nightly for one week about a problem they wanted to address. During that time, half of the students had a dream related specifically to their problem. Of these dreams, 70 percent offered a solution. The solutions came more often when the problems were personal rather than objective or academically oriented.[4]

I suggest the following steps for dream incubation that is specifically suited to bereavement dreaming:

1) While sitting quietly in meditation in front of your altar, pray for a dream that will help you with your grief, or for any other concern that you may have about yourself or your loved one. To be most effective, the request should be made with heartfelt emotion, rather than as an exercise of curiosity. An emotional investment and a trust in the outcome produce the best results. Ask the question you want the dream to address again shortly before retiring for the night, and then again just before falling to sleep.

You may long for an appearance of your loved one in a dream. It is appropriate to feel this way, but try not to demand or expect too much. To pressure your loved ones in this way creates an emotional conflict for them when they need to let go of their earthly attachments, just as you must begin the process of letting go of them. Jung, Sogyal Rinpoche, and the world-renowned medium Edgar Cayce warn of encouraging such contacts. Cayce says, "As much as we, the physical survivors, may crave such a contact, our continuing love requires patience. The best that we can do is to be open to receive such an experience—and diligent in trying to remember our dreams so that we can claim it should it come."[5] In the incubation process, pose a question or concern, and accept what comes to you. If your loved one does not appear, there may be an important reason for it. Healing comes in strange ways and is often what you least expect.

It is believed that dreams originate from the Self, or soul, the source within you that is an aspect of God. Address the request to this higher power and honor it with reverence and true compassion. Maximum benefit from your dreams comes when you have this proper relationship with the Self. It also helps to make a commitment that, when the dream is revealed, you will do something with it in a positive, meaningful way.

2) Whether or not you benefit from dream incubation depends, to some degree, on how you prepare yourself to receive the dream. Set a notebook or dream journal and a pen beside your bed so that, when you remember the dream, you will be able to record it immediately. Dreams are characteristically fleeting. They can be forgotten in an instant. Have a good night's sleep and let the dream induction go at this point. Sleep well with as few worries and concerns as possible so your unconscious can do its work uninterrupted.

3) Upon awakening, lie with your eyes closed and your attention focused inward, while exploring your unconscious for a dream or remnant of a dream. You may feel as if you must hurry along to start your day, but taking these few minutes can benefit you more than you realize. If time is of the essence, set your alarm a bit earlier to allow for this period of introspection and dream recording. Often, I've awoken with nothing in mind, and just taking these few moments brings immediate recall.

If something comes to your mind, record it and date it. Sometimes, just the process of writing a dream fragment brings more recall, until the entire dream returns to you. If only a few words about an image is all you have, however, that is good too. Honor whatever your unconscious has given to you.

Possibly, and this is not unusual, you may have no sense of a dream at all. In that case, your unconscious was not ready to register one. Trust that it will come, and do the incubation ritual again the next night. You may want to repeat the entire process in front of your altar; or, before retiring, remind yourself that you would like a dream to address your concern. Continue to do this night after night until you finally do receive a dream. I would not be surprised if you have one within a week of your initial request.

JOURNALING AND DREAM TENDING

Hopefully, within a short time, you will have a dream recorded in your bereavement dream journal, along with the date it occurred. It is ready and waiting there for you when you have a period of quiet time. Try to arrange this time as soon as possible, and not more than a day or two after you had the dream. The longer you wait, the more distant and less meaningful the dream will be for you. Its essence depends on your emotional energy and your willingness to be engaged with it.

Read the dream and ponder how you feel about it. Ponder also how you felt upon awakening, as well as how you felt while the dream was occurring. Your feelings in each of these states will provide clues to how consciously and unconsciously you are connected to the matter at hand. You may be disappointed that the dream doesn't seem to address your question or request. This is not unusual. Dreams speak metaphorically rather than directly, so that they often appear irrelevant and even a bit silly to your conscious mind. Most likely, however, it is more relevant than you realize. You will see this as you associate with the images.

Make a separate section in your journal for "dream tending" or "dream enlargements." Rewrite the dream again, if you like: give it a title and expand on some of the happenings and descriptions if more come to your mind as you write the dream. Select images and symbols that stand out in the dream and write more about them—associations that you have, and thoughts of past and present happenings that relate to them. Be sensitive to what feelings come to you as you write, especially when you have a deep "knowing" that you have connected with a particular meaning.

If your departed loved one is in the dream, take note of your interaction or lack of interaction with him or her. You may have been in the middle of a dialog when the dream was cut short or would like to have said something that you didn't get to say at the time. Now is the time to continue that dialog, right in your journal. Close your eyes, return to the setting, and allow yourself to experience again the feelings you had in the dream. Then begin your dialog. You may make a statement, express a feeling, or ask a question. Respond to this statement or question now from the point of view of your loved one. Some people prefer to switch writing hands at this point, with their dominant hand expressing their conscious attitude and the less dominant hand expressing the unconscious. If you normally use your right hand, use your left when speaking as your loved one. I find it easier to stay with one hand for both, but others say they feel differently when using the non-dominant hand. What's important is to do what is comfortable for you and to be engaged with your feelings and the process you are experiencing. Emotions may flow as you write, and that is good—continue to go deeply into your feelings. If you need to express regrets, sorrows, anger, or even tremendous joy, allow yourself to do so. Try not to judge—just let the feelings flow.

During your writing, your loved one may say things through you that are profound or strangely "out of the blue." Take in what is said and allow yourself to explore it more when the feelings have passed. You also may feel nothing meaningful at all from the writing experience. In that case, it may be too soon for you to go into the feelings or the matter at hand. Trust that it may not be the right time. Maybe later, through another dream, or when you feel more engaged in the process, it will come to you.

I will not go into dream interpretation here, since there are many good books on the subject. Some that I recommend include *A Little Course in Dreams* by Robert Bosnak, *Creative Dreaming* by Patricia Garfield, *Inner Work* by Robert Johnson, and *Dream Work* by Jeremy Taylor. When dream tending, processing, or interpreting, I suggest first exploring as much as you can from your personal associations, memories, and inherent knowledge. Try to get as emotionally involved with the images as you can. If you feel the urge to draw something from the dream, write a poem, or move to it physically, I encourage you to express yourself. This is the process of dream tending that can take you into many new dimensions of your soul, and into very healing grief work.

If, by chance, you are unable to make any personal connections at all with a particular image or an entire dream, you may be encountering a symbol or theme from the collective or universal realm of the unconscious. Such soul images require a bit of research in symbol dictionaries or mythological literature. I highly recommend *A Dictionary of Symbols* by J. E. Cirlot, and *The Women's Dictionary of Symbols and Sacred Objects* by Barbara Walker. Read all of the meanings to the symbol and be sensitive to what feels right for you and what makes the most sense in relation to what is happening to you in your current life. Be aware of meanings that are associated with death and near-death experiences, funerary rites, the afterlife, or mandalas and spiritual images. Because of your loss, your psyche is deeply enmeshed with death and all that is a part of it, especially within the first months or year following it. Trust what comes and allow yourself to be guided wherever the symbol takes you.

It is very important in dream interpretation to make certain that your ego is involved in the process at all times, as an observer and as a decision maker. Do not assume that the messages you receive are directly from the voice of God, or from your departed loved one who you assume is now knowledgeable about all things. The dream could very well come from your shadow (repressed or rejected contents of the psyche), a spoiling complex (neurotic tendencies), or even from an evil, collective source. It is not true that physical death suddenly bestows instant enlightenment. Do not automatically trust that your departed can now suddenly be your spirit guide without first exploring this from what you know or feel about him or her. This is especially true when he or she was not honest, wise, or caring when living.

Assess if the advice given to you in a dream, either in symbolic form or from your departed loved one, makes sense to you. Does it guide you in the direction of growth and healing? If not, the deceased may be in a negative frame, or it could be something negative within yourself that has taken on the appearance of your loved one. It's important to realize, as well, that passing from the earthly to the spiritual plane does not suddenly change the soul energy of the departed. Religious teachers, mediums, and even your dreams indicate that the state of the soul, whether negative or positive, light or dark, remains with the soul into the afterlife. Your knowledgeable, adult, and discriminative ego should always be the final decision maker on what does or does not appear to be right. Generally, you can trust dreams and the messages they bring you, but you must always be discriminative about them.

If by chance, you have no dream from the incubation process, the message or question you posed may be influencing you in ways of which you are unaware. Unremembered dreams may continue to affect you subliminally, so that thoughts during the day may suddenly come, as if out of the blue. Events in the outer world may also be affected by the happenings in the unconscious that result in synchronicities and chance encounters. Be sensitive to these outer events, opportunities, and sudden thoughts that appear. When you trust them and act on them, many wonderful things may happen in your life, in spite of the horrible loss you have suffered.

chapter ten

THE HERB OF RENEWAL

O soul, O spirit with me stay,
That I may greet the light of day.
Hero of peace, come forth from me,
Whom the whole world would like to see!

—VERUS HERMES, *Collected Works of C. G. Jung,* vol. 13

Hermes, most popular of the Greek gods, is revered as a source of luck to those who travel afar; but he is primarily a divine messenger from his father, Zeus, to mortals on Earth. Hermes, with his broad hat and winged sandals, is said to have carried a golden caduceus—a staff of writhing snakes—that he gave to Aesculapius, the god of healing. During his travels, Hermes is known to leave road markers, called "herms," as guides for travelers. These four-sided structures may be used as grave markers and can be found in our cemeteries today.[1] Little do we realize how much mythology influences our everyday life, habits, and rituals.

This messenger of the gods and guardian of the dead is also known as the god of our dreams. The ancient Greeks, well aware of the treasures and good fortune that he brought to them, prayed to Hermes to send them dreams for guidance and healing. Jung describes Hermes as "a spirit that penetrates into the depths of the material world and transforms it."[2] He points the way and reveals divine secrets to you. You do have to be aware of his trickster nature, however, which is why your ego must be involved when you work with your dreams. In fairytales, Hermes is the spirit in the bottle, an image you may well know from childhood.

Archetypal images of Hermes that are met by your conscious mind bring purpose and intentionality into your life. As seen in the previous dream stories, when your world is filled with chaos and pain, you are naturally drawn into the spaceless-timeless dimension of archetypal images. The archetypes are ordering principles that bring meaning, intentionality, and even destiny into the suffering that you experience. According to Jung, without conscious engagement with these archetypes in your dreams and fantasies, healing cannot take place very deeply.

The archetypal journey of transformation in the epic of Gilgamesh, a myth recorded four thousand years ago, still provides guidance today. The journey that Gilgamesh undertakes out of profound grief takes him to a secret of the gods—a plant that grows in the depths of the water, or the unconscious—a plant that sends forth "new life" to those who find it. To retrieve this herb, Gilgamesh ties rocks to his feet in order to go deep enough to find it. After bringing the plant up, Gilgamesh appears to fail in his task: while he bathes in the waters, a serpent takes the plant back into the depths and then it sheds its skin. Symbolically, such an outcome is not a failure, however. It is a transformation and renewal on the unconscious level. The hero-king, Gilgamesh, does not bring the "herb of renewed life" back to Uruk with him as he had planned. But he does return as a transformed man-king, who rules from his divine nature, rather than from the ineffective and uncaring drive of his former ego.

The four dreamers described in Part II journeyed into the depths of the unconscious where they, too, encountered many of life's mysterious forms that were presented in their dreams. In each dream series, they experienced at least one herb of renewal, revealed as an archetypal image with divine qualities. Contained within each image, were glimpses of the dreamer's destiny as well.

In one of Peter's dreams, he encounters his archetypal herb in a museum-like room into which he, like Gilgamesh, has to be lowered. Called "an inner, secret room" that Peter associates with his deceased brother, the room appears as a fateful calling to him long before his brother's death. In this room, Peter discovers "a most beautiful exhibit . . . of an upside down ivory tree, its roots up in the air with figures of . . . angels, naturally formed in the small, fine roots." A helper pulls Peter up from the room's depths after he encounters this profound archetypal image, and with him comes a basket containing several books and a colorfully ringed snake. Such a snake, an archetypal image of transformation and renewal, is often revealed during critical and transitional moments in your life. Books were a consistent symbol in many of Peter's dreams and, at least once, he said that he had thoughts of writing a book.

Sarah encounters her herb of renewed life in a dream she has while attending a retreat long before her son, John's, death. She is concerned at the time about the welfare of another son. Then, in tune with her ultimate fate, she is given an image that is "strong enough to hold *anything*"— a hammered, round, bronze platter. She knows that the image and message can give her the courage to bear whatever life brings to her. Sarah returns to her platter of solid strength again and again through her years of grief following John's death. The image helps her to become as strong and as solid as the bronze archetype projects. For Sarah, it is her symbol of transformation and herb of renewed life.

Experiencing a spiritual crisis in her dreams ushered in by the death of her young husband, Kevin, Kathleen is suddenly pulled into what seems like the inner light of heaven through the dimension of a huge eye. The intensity of that moment takes her breath away and remains with her long afterward in the outer world. Jung claims that, through such a process, "the intentions of the soul are made known to us" so that "all things take form."[3] It isn't long after encountering her unique herb of renewed life that Kathleen decides to return to her nursing studies to specialize, this time, on living and dying.

My herb of renewal does not come to me until I am in the throes of a mid-life crisis that begins with my disillusionment with marriage and family life many years after my son's death. While wondering what to do, I dream of entering a Jung Institute for couples therapy. Suddenly, I am drawn downward toward an orange-and-gold-ringed mandala that contains the rising of a wrapped mummy. Little do I know at the time that I will be writing a book about death, immortality, and transformation as part of my healing process.

A true story told through Self-Realization Fellowship, an international religious organization founded by Indian guru Paramahansa Yogananda, reveals the destined beginning of their world-famous Lake Shrine Temple on Sunset Boulevard in Los Angeles. In the early 1900s, a ten-acre parcel of land lay dormant as a worthless swamp, even though it contained the only natural spring-fed lake in the city of Los Angeles. Everett McElroy, assistant superintendent of construction for the 20th Century Fox studios, suddenly saw a vision of the hills surrounding the mud hole—terraces of trees, banks of flowers, and a pathway surrounding a beautiful lake that people from all over the world visited. He purchased the land, developed it to fit his vision, moved his Mississippi-style houseboat from Lake Mead to sit on the shoreline, and built an authentic reproduction of a 16th-century Dutch windmill. Movie stars and royalty retreated to this beautiful site and it was used in several movie productions.

Years later, McElroy sold his property to an oil magnate who had plans to develop it into a commercial enterprise. One night during his planning phase, the magnate had an intense dream that woke him in a profound state. He described the dream as dramatically vision-like with people from a "Church of All Religions" walking the pathway surrounding the lake and ministers speaking from a podium. The dream came to him not once, but three times during the night. Unable to sleep and driven with intense response to it, the oil magnate looked up "Church of All Religions" in the Los Angeles telephone directory. He found only one church listed: Self-Realization Fellowship Church of All Religions. The magnate immediately wrote a letter to its spiritual founder, Paramahansa Yogananda, offering to sell him his precious property. His wife woke up and berated him for what he was doing at three o'clock in the morning—trying to sell their home! Unperturbed, he finished the letter and mailed it. It is said that Yogananda had been anticipating an offer to purchase the property and was not surprised when it came to him.

Today, toward the end of Sunset Boulevard near the ocean, a beautiful, white shrine in the shape of a lotus flower dominates the scene. Many are awestruck and drawn to this mysterious sight when they see it. Below the temple shrine is the lake of all religions, the dream image and destined purpose of this wondrous place that was revealed to the oil magnate in his dream. He responded to the image that came to him with foresight, action, and generosity. Because he took his dream seriously and responded to it, millions of visitors each year walk the grounds of this spiritual site. Many are deeply touched and transformed in their encounter with the lake.

You never know what is in store for you when strange events or dreams come to you. You may not know if they are enlightening or tragic. Destiny, in one form or another, may be a large part of them, and if you are in tune with your dreams, you may certainly find that their calling comes from the depths of your soul.

NOTES

Introduction

1 J. D. Reed, "Across the Great Divide," *People Weekly* (Oct. 25, 1999): 116–126.

2 Aniela Jaffé, *Apparitions* (Irving, TX: Spring Publications, 1979).

3 Stephen Schuchter and Sidney Zisook, "The Course of Normal Grief," in Margaret and Wolfgang Stroebe and Robert Hansson, eds., *Handbook of Bereavement: Theory, Research and Intervention* (Cambridge: Cambridge University Press, 1993), p. 25.

Chapter 1

1 Alexander Heidel, *The Gilgamesh Epic and Old Testament Parallels*, 2nd edition (Chicago: University of Chicago Press, 1949), p. 55 f.

2 Heidel, *Gilgamesh Epic*, p. 57.

3 Heidel, *Gilgamesh Epic*, p. 63.

4 Quoted in Rivkah Schärf Kluger, *The Archetypal Significance of Gilgamesh: A Modern Ancient Hero* (Einsiedeln, Switzerland: Daimon Verlag, 1991), p. 160.

5 Heidel, *Gilgamesh Epic*, p. 64.

6 Heidel, *Gilgamesh Epic*, p. 90.

7 Heidel, *Gilgamesh Epic*, p. 66.

8 Kluger, *Archetypal Significance of Gilgamesh*, p. 165.

9 Kluger, *Archetypal Significance of Gilgamesh*, p. 171.

10 Heidel, *Gilgamesh Epic*, p. 91.

11 Heidel, *Gilgamesh Epic*, p. 91 f.

12 Kluger, *Archetypal Significance of Gilgamesh*, p. 207.

13 Kluger, *Archetypal Significance of Gilgamesh*, p. 159.

Chapter 2

1 Loring Danforth, *The Death Rituals of Rural Greece* (Princeton: Princeton University Press, 1982).

2 Danforth, *Death Rituals*.

3 Arnold Van Gennep, *The Rites of Passage* (Chicago: University of Chicago Press, 1960), p. 46.

4 Van Gennep, *The Rites of Passage*.

5 Grof is former Chief of Psychiatric Research at the Maryland Psychiatric Research Center and was influential in starting the transpersonal psychology movement. His work is primarily on the study of consciousness. It recognizes the spiritual aspect of the psyche.

6 Stanislav Grof, *Beyond the Brain* (Albany: State University of New York, 1985).

7 Grof, "Survival After Death," in Gary Doore, ed., *What Survives?* (Los Angeles: Jeremy P. Tarcher, 1990), pp. 22–33.

8 C. G. Jung, *Letters*, vol. I, R. F. C. Hull, trans. (Princeton: Princeton University Press, 1975), p. 257.

9 Edward Edinger, *Ego and Archetype* (Boston: Shambhala, 1992), p. 199. Von Franz states: "[O]ne feels compelled to leave them in space as a symbolic statement about another reality from which we are separated by a mysterious and dangerous barrier." Marie-Louise von Franz, *On Dreams and Death* (Boston: Shambhala, 1986), p. 157.

10 Edinger, *Ego and Archetype*, p. 200.

11 Sogyal Rinpoche, *The Tibetan Book of Living and Dying* (San Francisco: HarperSanFrancisco, 1994), p. 11.

12 Plutarch, *De sera numinis vindicta*, xxii, p. 564, quoted in von Franz, *On Dreams and Death*, p. 136.

13 Joel Martin and Patricia Romanowski, *Love Beyond Life: The Healing Power of After-Death Communications* (New York: HarperCollins, 1997), pp. 39–44.

14 C. G. Jung, *Memories, Dreams, Reflections* (New York: Vintage Books, 1961), p. 296.

Chapter 3

1 Carl Jung, *The Structure and Dynamics of the Psyche, The Collected Works of C. G. Jung*, vol. 8, R.F.C. Hull, trans. Bollingen Series XX (Princeton: Princeton University Press, 1970), ¶ 502. Further references to *The Collected Works* will be cited as *CW* with the volume number. Volume details are in the bibliography.

2 See full story in Joel Martin and Patricia Romanowski, *Love Beyond Life: The Healing Power of After-Death Communications* (New York: HarperCollins, 1997), p. 191.

3 C. G. Jung, *Letters*, vol. I, R.F.C. Hull, trans. (Princeton: Princeton University Press, 1975), p. 258.

4 Sogyal Rinpoche, *The Tibetan Book of Living and Dying* (San Francisco, CA: HarperSanFrancisco, 1994).

5 Marie-Louise von Franz, *On Dreams and Death* (Boston: Shambhala, 1986), p. 112.

6 Jung, *Letters*, vol. 2, p. 561.

7 Sogyal Rinpoche, *Tibetan Book of Living and Dying.*

8. Lily Pincus, *Death and the Family* (New York: Pantheon Books, 1974). See also Beverley Raphael, *The Anatomy of Bereavement* (New York: Basic Books Inc., 1983).

9 Verena Kast, *A Time to Mourn: Growing Through the Grief Process* (Einsiedeln, Switzerland: Daimon Verlag, 1982), p. 63.

10 Arnold Van Gennep, *The Rites of Passage* (Chicago: University of Chicago Press, 1960).

11 Stephen Schuchter and Sidney Zisook, "The Course of Normal Grief" in Margaret and Wolfgang Stroebe and Robert Hansson, eds., *Handbook of Bereavement* (Cambridge: Cambridge University Press, 1993).

12 Robert Romanyshyn, *The Soul in Grief* (Berkeley, CA: Frog Ltd., 1999), p. 31.

13 Raymond Moody, *Life After Life* (New York: Bantam Books, 1976), p. 31.

14 Von Franz, *On Dreams and Death*, p. 56.

15 E. A. Wallis Budge, *The Egyptian Book of the Dead: The Book of Going Forth by Day* (San Francisco: Chronicle Books, 1994), p. 149.

16 Von Franz, *On Dreams and Death.*

17 Robert Crookall, *"Dreams" of High Significance* (Moradabad, India: Darshana International, 1974), p. 63.

18 Crookall, *"Dreams" of High Significance*, p. 64.

19 Sogyal Rinpoche, *The Tibetan Book of Living and Dying*, p. 300.

20 Von Franz, *On Dreams and Death*, p. 53.

21 C. G. Jung, *Memories, Dreams, Reflections* (New York: Vantage Books, 1961), p. 294.

22 Jung, *CW* 14, ¶ 18.

23 Danforth, *The Death Rituals of Rural Greece.*

24 Sogyal Rinpoche, *The Tibetan Book of Living and Dying*, p. 291.

25 Crookall, *"Dreams" of High Significance*, p. 42.

26 John of the Cross, *Dark Night of the Soul* (Garden City, NY: Image Books, 1959), p. 111.

27 Jung, *CW* 5, ¶ 319.

28 John of the Cross, *Dark Night of the Soul* I, XII, p. 3.

29 Von Franz, *On Dreams and Death.*

30 John of the Cross, *Dark Night of the Soul*, pp. 176–180.

31 Kast, *A Time to Mourn*, p. 63.

32 Dierdre Barrett, "Through a Glass Darkly: Images of the Dead in Dreams," in *Omega: Journal of Death and Dying* 24, no. 2 (1992–1992): 92–108.

33 Martin and Romanowski, *Love Beyond Life*, p. 127.

34 Kast, *A Time to Mourn*, p. 65.

35 Jung, *Memories, Dreams, Reflections*, p. 315.

36 Jung, *Memories, Dreams, Reflections*, pp. 315–316.

37 Jung, *Memories, Dreams, Reflections*, p. 309.

38 Von Franz, *On Dreams and Death*, p. ix.

39 Jung, *Memories, Dreams, Reflections*, p. 308.

40 Ibid.

41 Sogyal Rinpoche, *The Tibetan Book of Living and Dying*, p. 299.

42 Kast, *A Time to Mourn*, p. 46.

43 Andrew Neher, *The Psychology of Transcendence* (Englewood Cliffs, NJ: Prentice-Hall, 1980).

44 Romanyshyn, *The Soul in Grief*, p. 119.

45 Neher, *The Psychology of Transcendence*, p. 131.

Chapter 4

1   C. G. Jung, *CW* 8.

2   Aniela Jaffé, *Apparitions and Precognition: A Study From the Point of View of C. G. Jung's Analytical Psychology* (New York: University Books, 1963), p. 24.

3   Sogyal Rinpoche, *The Tibetan Book of Living and Dying* (San Francisco: HarperSanFrancisco, 1994), p. 245.

4   Ad de Vries, *Dictionary of Symbols and Imagery* (Amsterdam: Elsevier Science Publishers, 1984).

5   E. Herzog, *Psyche and Death* (Dallas: Spring Publications,1983).

6   N. Micklem, "The Asklepian Myth" in *Harvest* 23 (1977): 27–38. A dream or vision of Aesculapius indicated to the sick that they were called by him and they would be healed.

7   Carl Meier, *Healing Dream and Ritual* (Einsiedeln, Switzerland: Daimon Verlag, 1989).

8   Marie-Louise von Franz, *On Dreams and Death* (Boston: Shambhala, 1986), p. 117.

9   Elisabeth Kübler-Ross, *On Children and Death* (New York: Macmillan, 1983).

10 D. S. Rogo, "Spontaneous Contact with the Dead," in Gary Doore, ed., *What Survives? Contemporary Explorations of Life After Death* (Los Angeles: Jeremy P. Tarcher, 1990).

11 Jung, *CW* 8, ¶ 814.

12 C. G. Jung, *Letters,* vol. I, R. F. C. Hull, trans. (Princeton: Princeton University Press, 1975), p. 117f.

13 Patricia Garfield, *The Dream Messenger* (New York: Simon and Schuster, 1997).

14 Stanislav Grof, Elisabeth Kübler-Ross, Raymond Moody, Marie-Louise von Franz.

15 Raymond Moody, *Reflections on Life After Life* (New York: Bantam Books, 1978), p. 9.

16 J. E. Cirlot, *Dictionary of Symbols* (New York: Philosophical Library, 1962), p. 76.

17 Von Franz, *On Dreams and Death.*

18 Thorwald Dethlefsen, *The Challenge of Fate* (London: Conventure, 1984), p. 154.

19 Patricia Dale-Green, *The Archetypal Cat* (Dallas: Spring Publications, 1963).

20 Von Franz, *On Dreams and Death.*

21 C. G. Jung, *Memories, Dreams, Reflections* (New York: Vintage Books, 1961), p. 301.

22 Jung, *Memories, Dreams, Reflections*, p. 302.

23 Cirlot, *A Dictionary of Symbols.*

24 Alfred Lord Tennyson, "Ulysses," in *Selected Poems* (London: Penguin Books, 1991), p. 95.

25 Random House Webster's College Dictionary.

26 Jung, *CW* 9i.

27 Verena Kast, *A Time to Mourn: Growing Through the Grief Process* (Einsiedeln, Switzerland: Daimon Verlag, 1982).

28 De Vries, *Dictionary of Symbols and Imagery.*

29 Barbara Hannah, *The Cat, Dog and Horse Lectures and "The Beyond"* (Wilmette, IL: Chiron Publications, 1992), p. 115.

Chapter 5

1 Marie-Louise von Franz, *On Dreams and Death* (Boston: Shambhala, 1986), p. 18.

2 Von Franz, *On Dreams and Death*, p. 94.

3 Von Franz, *On Dreams and Death*, p. 100.

4 Sogyal Rinpoche, *The Tibetan Book of Living and Dying* (San Francisco: HarperSanFrancisco, 1994).

5 Barbara Walker, *Women's Dictionary of Symbols and Sacred Objects* (San Francisco: HarperSanFrancisco, 1988), p. 305.

6 Ibid.

7 C. G. Jung, *CW* 13, ¶ 229.

8 Sogyal Rinpoche, *Tibetan Book of Living and Dying*, p. 301.

9 Sogyal Rinpoche, *Tibetan Book of Living and Dying*, p. 310.

10 C. G. Jung, *Memories, Dreams, Reflections*, p. 308.

11 Lily Pincus, *Death and the Family* (New York: Pantheon Books, 1974), p. 46.

12 De Vries, *Dictionary of Symbols and Imagery*, p. 202.

13 Walker, *Women's Dictionary of Symbols and Sacred Objects*, p. 121.

14 Cirlot, *Dictionary of Symbols.*

15 Walker, *Women's Dictionary of Symbols and Sacred Objects.*

16 Sogyal Rinpoche, *The Tibetan Book of Living and Dying,* p. 300.

17 Jung, *CW* 16, ¶ 479.

18 Sogyal Rinpoche, *The Tibetan Book of Living and Dying,* p. 311.

19 Stanislav Grof, *Beyond the Brain: Birth, Death, and Transcendence in Psychotherapy* (Albany: State University of New York, 1985), p. 100.

20 Jung, *CW* 12, ¶ 431.

21 Jung, *CW* 14, ¶ 46.

22 De Vries, *Dictionary of Symbols and Imagery.*

23 Cirlot, *Dictionary of Symbols,* p. 235.

24 Jung, *CW* 16, ¶ 507.

25 James Hollis, *Swamplands of the Soul* (Toronto: Inner City Books, 1996), p. 45.

26 Marie-Louise von Franz, "Archetypes Surrounding Death," in *Quadrant* 12, no. 1 (1979): 19.

27 Sogyal Rinpoche, *The Tibetan Book of Living and Dying,* p. 318.

Chapter 6

1   C. G. Jung, *CW* 9i, ¶ 11.

2   Jung, *CW* 9i, ¶ 714.

3   Joel Martin and Patricia Romanowski, *Love Beyond Life* (New York: HarperCollins, 1997).

4   Sogyal Rinpoche, *The Tibetan Book of Living and Dying* (San Francisco: HarperSanFrancisco, 1994).

5   Barbara Walker, *The Women's Dictionary of Symbols and Sacred Objects* (San Francisco: HarperSanFrancisco, 1988), p. 418.

6   Patricia Garfield, *The Dream Messenger* (New York: Simon & Schuster, 1997).

7   Linda Leonard, *Creation's Heartbeat* (New York: Bantam Books, 1995).

8   Leonard, *Creation's Heartbeat,* p. 67.

9   James Hollis, *Swamplands of the Soul* (Toronto: Inner City Books, 1996), pp. 32–33.

10 Jung, *CW* 14, ¶ 732.

11 E. A. Wallis Budge, *Osiris, the Egyptian Religion of Resurrection,* vol. II, reprinted (New Hyde Park, NY: University Books, 1961), p. 355, quoted in Edward Edinger, *Ego and Archetype* (Boston: Shambhala, 1992), p. 213.

Chapter 7

1 Caitlin Matthews, *Sophia* (London: Aquarian, 1992), p. 37.
2 C. G. Jung, *CW* 5, ¶ 553.
3 Jung, *CW* 5, ¶ 421.
4 Jung, *CW* 13, ¶ 462.
5 A. C. Bhaktivedanta Swami Prabhupada, *Bhagavad-Gita* (Los Angeles: Bhaktivedanta Book Trust, 1990), p. 711.
6 Swami Prabhupada, *Bhagavad-Gita,* p. 538.
7 Jung, *CW* 13, ¶ 462.
8 Alexander Heidel, *The Gilgamesh Epic and Old Testament Parallels* (Chicago: University of Chicago Press, 1949), p. 91 f.
9 James Hillman, *The Soul's Code* (New York: Random House, 1996), p. 8.

Chapter 8

1 Sogyal Rinpoche, *The Tibetan Book of Living and Dying* (San Francisco: HarperSanFrancisco, 1994).
2 C. G. Jung, *CW* 9i, ¶ 246.
3 Jung, *CW* 9i, ¶ 248.
4 Jung, *CW* 9i, ¶ 241.

Chapter 9

1 Joel Covitz, *Visions of the Night: A Study of Jewish Dream Interpretation* (Boston: Shambhala, 1990).
2 Judy Tatelbaum, *The Courage to Grieve* (New York: Lippincott & Crowell, 1980), p. 9.
3 Sogyal Rinpoche, *The Tibetan Book of Living and Dying* (San Francisco: HarperSanFrancisco, 1993), p. 300.
4 Deidre Barrett, "The 'Committee of Sleep:' A Study of Dream Incubation for Problem Solving," in *Dreaming: Journal of the Association for the Study of Dreams* 3 no. 2 (June, 1993): 115–122.

5   Mark Thurston, *Edgar Cayce's Wisdom for the Ages: Dreams* (San Francisco: Harper & Row, 1988), p. 102.

Chapter 10

1   David A. Leeming, *The World of Popular Myth* (New York: Oxford University Press, 1990).

2   C. G. Jung, *CW* 11, ¶ 356.

3   Jung, *CW* 14, ¶ 46.

BIBLIOGRAPHY

Aeschylus. *The Oresteia.* Ted Hughes, trans. New York: Farrar, Straus, Giroux, 1999.

Barrett, Deirdre. "The 'Committee of Sleep': A Study of Dream Incubation for Problem Solving." In *Dreaming: Journal of the Association for the Study of Dreams* 3, no. 2 (1993): 115–122.

———. "Through a Glass Darkly: Images of the Dead in Dreams." In *Omega: Journal of Death and Dying* 24, no. 2 (1991-1992): 92–108.

Budge, E. A. Wallis. *The Egyptian Book of the Dead: The Book of Going Forth by Day.* San Francisco: Chronicle Books, 1994.

———. *Osiris, The Egyptian Religion of Resurrection.* New Hyde Park, New York: University Books, 1961.

Bulkeley, Kelly. *Spiritual Dreaming: A Cross-cultural and Historical Journey.* New York: Paulist Press, 1995.

Cirlot, J. E. *A Dictionary of Symbols.* New York: Philosophical Library, 1962.

Covitz, Joel. *Visions of the Night: A Study of Jewish DreamInterpretation.* Boston: Shambhala, 1990.

Crookall, Robert. *"Dreams" of High Significance.* Moradabad, India: Darshana International, 1974.

Dale-Green, Patricia. *The Archetypal Cat.* Dallas: Spring Publications, 1963.

Danforth, Loring M. *The Death Rituals of Rural Greece.* Princeton: Princeton University Press, 1982.

Dethlefsen, Thorwald. *The Challenge of Fate.* London: Coventure, 1984.

De Vries, Ad. *Dictionary of Symbols and Imagery.* Amsterdam: Elsevier Science Publishers, 1984.

Edinger, Edward. *Ego and Archetype*. Kendra Crossen, ed. Boston: Shambhala, 1992.

Garfield, Patricia. *The Dream Messenger: How Dreams of the Departed Bring Healing Gifts*. New York: Simon and Schuster, 1997.

Gibran, Kahlil. *The Prophet*. New York: Alfred A. Knopf, 1973.

Graves, Robert. *Collected Poems*. Garden City, NY: Doubleday, 1958.

Grof, Christina and Stanislav. *The Stormy Search for the Self: A Guide to Personal Growth through Transformational Crisis*. Los Angeles: Jeremy P. Tarcher, 1990.

Grof, Stanislav. *Beyond the Brain: Birth, Death and Transcendence in Psychotherapy*. Albany: State University of New York, 1985.

Hannah, Barbara. *The Cat, Dog and Horse Lectures and "The Beyond."* D. Frantz, ed. Wilmette, IL: Chiron Publications, 1992.

Heidel, Alexander. *The Gilgamesh Epic and Old Testament Parallels*. Chicago: University of Chicago Press, 1949.

Herzog, Edgar. *Psyche and Death: Death-demons in Folklore, Myths and Modern Dreams*. Dallas: Spring Publications, 1983.

Hillman, James. *The Soul's Code: In Search of Character and Calling*. New York: Random House, 1996.

Hollis, James. *Swamplands of the Soul*. Toronto: Inner City Books, 1996.

Jaffé, Aniela. *Apparitions: An Archetypal Approach to Death, Demons and Ghosts*. Irving, TX: Spring Publications, 1979.

John of the Cross. *Dark Night of the Soul*. Garden City, NY: Image Books, 1959.

Jung, C. G. *Alchemical Studies. The Collected Works of C. G. Jung*, vol. 13. R.F.C. Hull, trans. Bollingen Series XX. Princeton: Princeton University Press, 1968.

———. *The Archetypes and the Collective Unconscious. The Collected Works of C. G. Jung*, vol. 9i. R.F.C. Hull, trans. Bollingen Series XX. Princeton: Princeton University Press, 1969.

———. *Letters*, vol. 1: 1906-1950 and vol. 2: 1951-1961. R. F. C. Hull, trans. Princeton: Princeton University Press, 1975.

———. *Memories, Dreams, Reflections*. New York: Vintage Books, 1961.

———. *Mysterium Coniunctionis. The Collected Works of C. G. Jung*, vol. 14. R.F.C. Hull, trans. Bollingen Series XX. Princeton: Princeton University

Press, 1974.

———. *The Practice of Psychotherapy. The Collected Works of C. G. Jung*, vol. 16. R.F.C. Hull, trans. Bollingen Series XX. Princeton: Princeton University Press, 1966.

———. *Psychology and Alchemy. The Collected Works of C. G. Jung*, vol. 12. R.F.C. Hull, trans. Bollingen Series XX. Princeton: Princeton University Press, 1980.

———. *Psychology and Religion: West and East. The Collected Works of C. G. Jung*, vol. 11. R.F.C. Hull, trans. Bollingen Series XX. Princeton: Princeton University Press, 1970.

———. *The Structure and Dynamics of the Psyche. The Collected Works of C. G. Jung*, vol. 8. R.F.C. Hull, trans. Bollingen Series XX. Princeton: Princeton University Press, 1970.

———. *Symbols of Transformation. The Collected Works of C. G. Jung*, vol. 5. R.F.C. Hull, trans. Bollingen Series XX. Princeton: Princeton University Press, 1977.

Kast, Verena. *A Time to Mourn: Growing through the Grief Process*. Einsiedeln, Switzerland: Daimon Verlag, 1982.

Kluger, Rivkah Schärf. *The Archetypal Significance of Gilgamesh: A Modern Ancient Hero*. Einsiedeln, Switzerland: Daimon Verlag, 1991.

Kübler-Ross, Elisabeth. *On Children and Death*. New York: Macmillan, 1983.

Leeming, David Adams. *The World of Myth: An Anthology*. New York: Oxford University Press, 1990.

Leonard, Linda Schierse. *Creation's Heartbeat: Following the Reindeer Spirit*. New York: Bantam Books, 1995.

Martin, Joel and Patricia Romanowski. *Love Beyond Life: The Healing Power of After-Death Communications*. New York: HarperCollins, 1997.

Matthews, Caitlin. *Sophia: Goddess of Wisdom*. London: Aquarian Press, 1992.

Meier, Carl A. *Healing Dream and Ritual*. Einsiedeln, Switzerland: Daimon Verlag, 1989.

Micklem, Neil. "The Asklepian Myth." In *Harvest: Journal for Jungian Studies* 23 (1977): 27–38.

Moody, Raymond. *Life after Life*. New York: Bantam Books, 1976.

———. *Reflections on Life after Life*. New York: Bantam Books, 1978.

Neher, Andrew. *The Psychology of Transcendence*. Englewood Cliffs, NJ: Prentice-Hall, 1980.

Neruda, Pablo. *The Captain's Verses*. New York: New Directions Publishing Corp., 1972.

Pincus, Lily. *Death and the Family*. New York: Pantheon Books, 1974.

Prabhupada, A. C. Bhaktivedanta Swami. *Bhagavad-Gita As It Is*. Los Angeles: The Bhaktivedanta Book Trust, 1990.

Raphael, Beverly. *The Anatomy of Bereavement*. New York: Basic Books, 1983.

Reed, J. D. "Across the Great Divide." In *People Weekly* (Oct. 25, 1999): 116–126.

Rogo, D. Scott. "Spontaneous Contact with the Dead: Perspectives from Grief Counseling, Sociology, and Parapsychology." In Gary Doore, ed. *What Survives? Contemporary Explorations of Life after Death*. Los Angeles: Jeremy P. Tarcher, 1990.

Romanyshyn, Robert. *The Soul in Grief*. Berkeley, CA: Frog Ltd., 1999.

Schuchter, Stephen and Sidney Zisook. "The Course of Normal Grief." In Margaret and Wolfgang Stroebe and Robert Hansson, eds. *Handbook of Bereavement: Theory, Research and Intervention*. Cambridge: Cambridge University Press, 1993.

Sogyal Rinpoche. *The Tibetan Book of Living and Dying*. San Francisco: HarperSanFrancisco, 1994.

Tatelbaum, Judy. *The Courage to Grieve*. New York: Lippincott & Crowell, 1980.

Tennyson, Alfred Lord. "Ulysses." In *Selected Poems*. London: Penguin Books, 1991.

Thurston, Mark. *Edgar Cayce's Wisdom for the Ages: Dreams*. San Francisco: Harper & Row, 1988.

Van Gennep, Arnold. *The Rites of Passage*. Chicago: University of Chicago Press, 1960.

Von Franz, Marie-Louise. *On Dreams and Death*. Boston & London: Shambhala, 1986.

———. "Archetypes Surrounding Death." In *Quadrant* 12, no. 1 (1970).

Walker, Barbara. *The Women's Dictionary of Symbols and Sacred Objects*. San Francisco: HarperSanFrancisco, 1988.

Whitman. Walt. *Leaves of Grass*. Harold Blodgett, ed. New York: New York University Press, 1965

Yogananda, Paramahansa. *God Talks with Arjuna: The Bhagavad Gita: Royal Science of God-realization*. Los Angeles: Self-Realization Fellowship, 1999.

INDEX

photo by Mary Kay Coleman

ABOUT THE AUTHOR

G eri Grubbs, Ph.D., wife, mother, and grandmother, is also a practicing Jungian analyst in the town of Woodinville, Washington. She is a graduate of the C. G. Jung Institute in Zurich and is a board member of the North Pacific Institute for Analytical Psychology. She has been practicing depth psychology since 1987 and is an experienced workshop and seminar leader. In addition to working with adults experiencing life in transition, spiritual crises, bereavement, and other emotional problems, she works with children and families.